NAMED JOEY

Joseph Kempston

A KID NAMED JOEY
© Copyright 2020 by Joe Kempston.
All rights reserved.

No part of this book may be reproduced or transmitted in any form or by any means, electronic or mechanical, including photocopying, recording, or by any information storage and retrieval system—except by a reviewer who may quote brief passages in a review to be printed in a magazine, newspaper, or on the WEB—without permission in writing from the author.

First Printing 2020

ISBN: 978-0-578-22970-6

Cover & Interior Design and Typesetting by Josh Pritchard.

To Joe and Olga, Dad and Mom, who taught me about goodness, kindness, love, loyalty, hard work, fun, forgiveness, and responsibility. I thank God for the two of them almost every day.

TABLE OF CONTENTS

Prologue 1

Chapter 1: Bikes, BB guns and Baseball 5

Chapter 2: Joey in Junior High — The Good,
    the Bad, the Mischievous 35

Chapter 3: Clover Park, Where Days are Brightest 65

Chapter 4: Dawg Days 89

Chapter 5: My Year of Sunshine 129

Epilogue 159

Prologue

WHEN THE DEPRESSION HIT in October 1929, my Grandpa and Grandma Kempston were living in Chicago. Like almost every family in America, they were impacted severely, and had to make some drastic changes to survive. As a result, in 1935 they made a gutsy move to Oregon to begin all over again. They were both 48. For a year, Grandpa stayed in Chicago to close down what was left of their former thriving business, while Grandma drove herself and the three kids still living at home to the Lorane Valley of Oregon, where she and Grandpa had just purchased a shack and forty acres for $900. She bought some laying hens and planted a cash crop of strawberry plants. Within months she was selling eggs and fresh strawberries. And they began anew. When Grandpa was able to join the family, he built a big house for $1500 using all kinds of used and scrounged materials and they were on their way. Their story is a story of resilience shared by many in that decade.

As Grandma was driving out to Oregon from Chicago, her car broke down in the middle of nowhere—a scene reminiscent of the Joad family in Steinbeck's *Grapes of Wrath*. She didn't know what to do, but being a woman who possessed a deep faith in God, immediately prayed and asked Him to rescue them. Shortly thereafter someone came along, stopped, and fixed the car. If Grandma were alive today, I would ask her so many questions about what exactly happened and more about her life at that time. Who stopped? Where exactly were they? Did she ever wonder if it was an angel? What was it like starting all over again? How many rows of strawberries did you plant? How did you meet Grandpa originally, anyway? And on and on.

So many times I've wished I'd been more interested in my grandparents' and parents' stories and delved into them when they were still living. I know a lot about them, but there is so much that I never learned. I have all these unanswered questions. One of my grandpas came to the US from Sweden; the other from Ireland. One of my grandmas emigrated from England. The other was a direct descendant of Benjamin Franklin's brother, Tom. I'd love to know what their early lives were like. And I've got so many questions I would ask Mom and Dad—questions that didn't occur to me to ask them when they were living. This is why I decided to write the story of my growing-up years, so my kids and grandkids can read it someday and know more than just an isolated story or two about their dad's or grandpa's early life. We're all connected, and that connection is important.

I was born November 2, 1941, a month and five days before the attack on Pearl Harbor brought the US into World War Two. My older sisters were four years old and 17 months old. At the time Dad was an army lieutenant stationed at Ford Ord on California's Monterey Peninsula. I was born in the artsy and picturesque little town of Carmel-by-the-Sea where they rented a home. During the war years, we moved around a bit as Dad's duty stations changed. From Carmel, we moved to the Presidio in San Francisco, then to Salt Lake City, and then to Bountiful, Utah. When Dad was discharged as a major in the spring of 1946, we spent a year on a ranch in Oregon, and then moved to Tacoma a year later where I grew up. And that's where my story begins. I hope you enjoy it.

CHAPTER 1
Bikes, BB guns, and Baseball

I CAN'T REMEMBER WHY, BUT I was mad at Butch Raudenbush, the kid who lived next door. Conveniently for my eight-year-old devious mind, a horse had gone by on the street and left a pile right in front of their mailbox. It was so fresh it was steaming. Without wasting any time, I got a little shovel and crammed that mailbox totally full of horse poop. As I was finishing the job, grinning wickedly to myself, I heard the crunch of tires in the gravel right behind me. I turned around, and saw Butch's dad. He rolled down his car window and calmly asked, "Joey, what in the world do you think you are doing?" Caught in the act, I reached in with my bare hand and started scooping the poop all out, apologizing all over the place and promising that I would never do it again. Without saying a word he drove up his driveway and I went in our house where I listened with my heart pounding for his phone call or his footsteps on the porch to tell my Mom. He never came, never phoned and never mentioned it again. I always liked the man after that. It was an experience in mercy I've never forgotten. Mercy was to play out many times in my growing up years, even though I rarely recognized it at the time.

I loved my growing up years. For me, being a kid in the 1940's and 1950's was a joyous combination of adventure, learning, and freedom. There were bikes, BB guns, and baseball; forts, fireworks, and friends — and always, family. I had the enviable good fortune to grow up in a family where warmth, love, and nurture were part of everyday life. Dad and Mom loved each other and every day I got to observe that mutual affection and respect playing out in all our lives. Each night as we kids went to bed, Dad or Mom, sometimes both, would come in our room and we'd hear those good words, "Good night. I love you."

In April 1947 my family moved from a 480 acre ranch outside Lorane, Oregon, to Tacoma, Washington. I was five. Dad had worked that ranch for only one year, after his discharge from the army at the end of World War Two. It had been his dream throughout the war to own and work his own ranch. He'd put money down and been making payments on the ranch all during the war years. The ranch boasted a decrepit farmhouse complete with outhouse, a barn which was on its last legs and which we were forbidden to enter, an ancient fruit house, sixty head of cattle, a creek, a fruit orchard and a vegetable garden. As hard as he tried, Dad wasn't able to make ends meet, and further, his back was giving him constant pain. He had injured it on one of our stateside moves during the war, and so, he had back surgery, sold the ranch, and took a job as a civilian running the quartermaster (supply) office for Fort Lewis. Thus, our move to Tacoma.

We stayed at a motel for a week or so on old 99, or Pacific, as we called it, before we moved into our house. The motel had a spruce tree in its front yard and a huge sign next door to it advertising Cutty Sark, with a big sailing ship on it. We ate our meals at a restaurant nearby.

Moving day arrived and we settled into what would be our family's home for the next six years. 6517 Steilacoom Blvd SW in the Lakewood suburb of Tacoma. We bought it from a family named the Drinkwines. We always chuckled about that name, wondering the obvious. Built in 1926, it was a small house on a long, narrow one acre lot with huge Douglas fir trees in the immediate backyard. Beyond those trees was a clearing with a beginning cluster of baby fir trees on one side. My parents paid $7000 for the property. The house sat at the front of the lot. There was a small garage with a woodshed in the back, and no lawn, just dirt and weeds.

I remember two things about moving day. I found a tiny green fake Christmas tree in the bathroom cabinet, and a neighbor boy from two houses away came over to see us. I was five and he was three. His name was JL. We became good friends and would play a lot together during our years there. His family had moved from Shreveport, Louisiana, and the funny thing about JL was that he called his mom and dad by their first names, Tom and MaryAnn. I thought if he did that, it must be okay, so I called my Mom "Olga" one day instead of Mom, and she let me know that wasn't okay. I was to call her "mother" or "mom."

The neighbors on one side were an older couple, the Dickinsons. I didn't know this until many years later, but Mr. Dickinson drank a lot. I always thought he was just a jolly old guy who told great stories. They had a pair of cute Boston terriers. On the other side lived another older couple, the Raudenbushes. Ruth Raudenbush was a kind lady who was interested in us and loved to garden. Her grandson was Butch, whose family lived there with them for one year. JL and his family lived on the other side of Raudenbushes. Across the street lived various families, often military, who seemed to move in and out a lot because of the proximity of Fort Lewis and McChord Air Force Base.

Because McChord AFB was the home for a squadron of C-119's, we'd often see them flying over our house as they went into their landing pattern. We were a few miles from the base, so they weren't flying at super low altitudes, but they made a lot of noise. I would find out later that they were cargo planes, nicknamed "Flying Boxcars." Because World War Two had ended only two years before and I had a big imagination, whenever I saw one I'd keep it in the corner of my eye to make sure it wasn't an enemy bomber. I would always figure out where I would run to if I saw bombs being dropped.

Right off the bat, life changed for me in that the state of Washington had kindergarten, while Oregon had not. Mom enrolled my sisters and me at Park Lodge Elementary School—Pat in the fourth grade, Judy in first, and me in afternoon kindergarten. The principal was Mrs.

Payne, but she wasn't a pain. She was nice. That spring, I attended four weeks of afternoon kindergarten—17 days according to my report card. The highlight of each day was walking 25 minutes in the early afternoon with Mom to school. It was a good hike, first on some streets, then over a big hill on a path through a field, then on some more streets and then we'd arrive. Mom was always such good company. We'd converse the entire time. I really liked that shared walk and I sensed that she did, too. It was the kind of time which makes you feel close to someone. She'd then walk the mile back home and I'd be there in kindergarten with my first-ever classmates and Mrs. Jones, the teacher.

My first day at kindergarten I played cars outside during afternoon recess with Gary Thomas and Charlie Bergeron. I would go through all of my school years with these two. They ended up being two of the best basketball players on our high school team, and Charlie was our senior class president. They are still friends of mine. The only other thing I remember is putting together a big puzzle one day when it was too rainy to go outside for recess. Just when I'd put the last piece together and the puzzle was complete, a mean girl came along and messed it all up on purpose. Being Mr. Sensitive, I cried.

Years later, my Mom gave me all my report cards that she'd saved through the years. The kindergarten one didn't have grades. It was just a form with a statement at the bottom which said, "I think Joey will be an average student. His being so young is his big drawback." I was glad Mom never shared that with me. Neither of us would have believed it anyway because I already knew how to read, and by the second grade, I was getting all "A's."

I loved first grade. My teacher was Miss O'Donnell, who was young and pretty. That year I got the measles and chicken pox and was absent for 30 days total. Missing those days didn't seem to bother me much because on the day I returned, I filled in my reading workbook without first reading the book. I just guessed on the answers. Hey, it worked. At least I never got called on it. Maybe that's where I picked up the habit of if you don't know how to do something, just fake it until you do. I also had difficulty in keeping jars of paste in my desk due to a newly acquired taste for it. Loved the stuff. I'd pull my jar of Elmer's paste out a couple of times a day, stick my finger in it and lick it off. Mmm.

The highlight of first grade for me happened one Friday night at the local ice skating rink on Steilacoom Lake not too far from our house. Dad had taken Judy and me skating there that night and as I was teetering around the ice, I heard a familiar voice behind me. "Hi Joey! Nice to see you here." It was Miss O'Donnell. She must have been a good skater because she was wearing one of those short skirts which women skaters sometimes wore back in the day. Well, pretty soon the lights dimmed and the sign changed from "All skate" to "Couples only" and because I had told my dad that my teacher was there, he asked her to skate. He was really a good skater, and

I remember feeling so proud that my dad was skating with my teacher. It was one of those fun, unexpected moments when your school life suddenly intersects with your home life and it seems a little surreal.

One embarrassing moment with Miss O'Donnell happened as I was leaving for home at the end of a school day. As I walked past her desk toward the door I waved and said, "Good night, Miss O'Donnell, I love you." Oops, force of habit. I turned red and hoped she hadn't heard, but when I looked back she was smiling. Probably happens to a lot of kids. Once.

When I had the measles and the chicken pox that year, I got to stay home with Mom all day, and I loved it. She'd fix me up in her bed, bring me meals and buy me special kids' game books—connect the dots kind of things. She bought an illustrated comic book of the Old Testament in the Bible, and I read through it twice. Because it was a real adventure, I began reading the actual Old Testament from the King James Version. That's the version most folks read in those days. I read it from Genesis through II Kings during one of those illnesses.

My next-oldest sister, Judy, was 17 months older than me, and a year ahead of me in school. We spent a lot of time together. Judy was a quick learner and athletic. She learned how to blow bubbles from bubble gum before I did, how to ride a bike before I did. And how to whistle. I did better in school kinds of things, but she did better in everything else. Park Lodge Elementary School only went up through the fourth grade. The school had an all-star baseball team which played other schools. Ours was composed of fourth graders and in that era, all guys, at least until Judy came along. She not only was the only girl on the team, she was also the pitcher, and the best batter. In one game she was pitching, Judy fielded a grounder from the batter but then overthrew the first baseman by a couple of feet, hitting our principal, Mrs. Payne.

Judy got a bike before I did. In the second grade, I got a quarter a week for an allowance and I decided to save for a bicycle. By the end of the school year I had accumulated $12. So Dad put $30 more with it and bought me a brand new J. C. Higgins red and white 24-inch bike for $42 from Sears and Roebuck.

After that, Judy and I hit the road together all the time. We had a friend named Neal Dempsey, who lived down on the corner, and often Neal would go with us. We biked on trails through the woods, we biked on backroads and main roads. We went everywhere. We biked to friend's houses. We'd ride down to the end of John Dower Road, where we thought a famous burglar nicknamed "Tapeface" lived in a scary cabin in the woods. We'd bicycle down Steilacoom Blvd to the brush and sage next to the state's mental hospital, Western State. In the fifth and sixth grades we cycled a mile on busy Steilacoom Blvd every morning and afternoon, rain or shine, to and from Navy Base School. The bikes gave us a wonderful sense of freedom. We were never bored. In fact, I never even learned that word until the sixth grade. In summers and on Saturdays during the school year we'd disappear until lunch, and after lunch, we'd pull the same routine until dinner. We'd let Mom know generally where we were going, but not always. If we were in the neighborhood somewhere, and it was lunch or dinner time, Mom had this distinctive whistle she would do. It had some vibrato to it. If one of our friends heard it first, they'd tell us that our mom was calling.

We used to pedal down to Chambers Creek, which flowed out of Steilacoom Lake into Puget Sound. There were a couple of ways to get there, but it was always an adventure. We'd run into garter snakes, nettles, and, at certain times of the year, spawning salmon. Once I found a big dead salmon and brought it home to Mom hoping she could cook it for dinner. Made me feel really proud, like I was contributing to the family meals. It was tough carrying that fish carcass home on my bike because it was so big and slippery. My feeling of pride didn't last long, however because Mom wasn't real happy about me bringing this stinking dead fish into her kitchen and told me to take it to the back woods and bury it.

Judy and I would make "forts" in different places—sometimes on our property, sometimes in the woods nearby. A fort had to be a secret place that nobody else knew about. We had rules for membership in one of the forts, which we still have a copy of. Rule #1. You have to have a knife. Rule # 2. Be ye kind, one to another. (Or else the first fort member would use their knife on you?) Judy remembers that we constructed one fort out of an old Texaco gas station sign which we'd found. We also collected bottle caps from pop bottles. I'll bet we had five or six hundred of them. Don't remember how we started that, but it gave us something to look for on our bike rides.

I mentioned Neal Dempsey. Neal was in my grade. He was a good friend and a really good guy — always loyal. Neal taught us all the sports—baseball, football, basketball, and later, golf. Neal eventually became an extremely successful venture capitalist, and a most generous one. He ended up being a large donor to the University of Washington, and two buildings on today's campus are named after him. We had a baseball diamond in our yard way in the back. Dad had bought some army surplus screen doors from Fort Lewis and made a backstop for us. A home run was anything over the back rundown fence. Mostly we'd play workup. Judy and Neal hit a lot of homers. I didn't. But I developed a skill for always getting a single or double, and I could place hit pretty accurately. So on our fifth and sixth grade school teams, and later in college on intramural teams, I was always chosen to bat leadoff. Summer nights in the Pacific Northwest were very long, and if we were playing after dinner, we could play till after nine most nights. We loved it. Neal was a southpaw and had a beautiful first baseman's glove. I didn't have a glove in those days, but when Neal was up to bat I'd borrow his glove and put it on my left hand backwards and it worked well. Judy was the only one in our family who had a baseball glove.

We'd play football in Neal's yard. Two on two or three

on three. Once I blocked Pete, Neal's little brother, too hard and broke his collarbone. He wasn't very happy about that. Forty years later, I was running with Neal in Monterey, California, and we were reminiscing a little, talking about his parents and mine, and growing up there in the same neighborhood. He said to me something which I've never forgotten—"Joe, you do know that your family was really special, don't you?" That's something I hadn't realized at the time, but that Neal had noticed. And I sure realized it as I grew older.

Neal also turned Judy and me on to major league baseball. In the early 1950's the New York Yankees were consistently the best team in the American League and often battled against the Brooklyn Dodgers of the National League in the World Series. He and Judy always favored the Yankees, but I had chosen to be a Dodger fan. Jackie Robinson had just broken the racial barrier and was playing for the Dodgers, and Yogi Berra was the star catcher for the Yankees. Summer afternoons, if I didn't have anything else to do, I'd sometimes sit by the radio and listen to a game.

Judy and I had a tendency to hurt ourselves. July fourth was a noisy time of blowing up all kinds of stuff with firecrackers. We'd put one under an ant pile and watch it blow. We'd find old pipes and stick regular firecrackers inside of them to make the boom sound louder. Once Judy was up on Neal's garage roof (we often sat up there and talked) and she lit a cherry bomb, but it didn't go off. So she climbed off the roof to see why, picked it up and it went off in her hand. It really hurt! Neither of us ever forgot that. But she was tough and didn't cry.

Next door in the very back of Dickinson's yard was a huge pile of logs. Mr. Dickinson had done some logging on the property and the logs were still there, piled about ten or twelve feet high. Judy and I would sometimes climb to the top of that pile just to sit and talk. Since it seemed so high, one day we got to talking about the idea of flying. We wondered if we flapped our arms really hard and jumped off, could we fly for even a short ways. Judy tried first. It didn't go well. Somehow she landed on her back and hurt herself. After seeing her flop, I opted out.

After school Judy and I and Neal would often walk down to King's Drugstore, just a block up the street, sit on the stools at their soda fountain and drink cokes. A coca cola was a nickel, and Judy always seemed to have a spare nickel for me when I was broke. My favorites were lime cokes and cherry cokes.

One time after enjoying a coke Neal and I had gone out the front door of the drugstore first. Two boys who were a grade younger but much bigger than we were, started to pick on us. One of them had just shoved me when Judy came out the door and saw what was going on. Because I knew her so well, I waited to see what she would do. She came up behind the big kid who'd just given me the shove, and punched him the back really hard. He got this totally surprised look on his face and fell over toward me, his breath gone. She stood over him and told him in no uncertain terms that if he or his friend ever picked on us again, they would regret it. They both bicycled off as Neal and I grinned at each other.

Dad was my hero. His name was Joe and his dad was named Joe, so I was the third one in a series of three. He always called me his pal. It seemed to me that he could do anything. One Saturday I saw him in the front yard with a shovel. He was turning over the dirt in the yard one shovelful at a time, working in long rows from left to right. After a couple of hours he had turned over all the dirt in the front yard, and he proceeded to the side and back yard to do the same thing. By the end of the day, he had raked it all and smoothed it over. He let me help with the raking. Then he rolled a huge concrete culvert pipe over it to tamp it down, threw out some seed, raked it in, and asked me to help him keep it wet over the next three weeks. Pretty soon the lawn sprouted, and he built a really nice white picket fence, a sidewalk and gate for the front. The place was transformed. Sometimes I'd ask him what he was doing and he would explain it all. He always let me help. To this day, when I've been out working in the yard for hours and all sweaty with a backache, I think of Dad, who really taught me how to work, and I smile and thank God for him.

He built a rope swing in the back yard which swung from a high branch of one of the big Douglas firs. I often wondered how he got up there to tie the rope in the first place. On another Douglas fir he constructed the coolest tree fort. We were the only kids within miles with a tree house like that one. Once, we went down to Chambers Creek and brought back buckets of mud and had a good old mud ball fight with attackers and defenders of the tree fort.

Dad was versatile. He cut my hair every other Saturday night. He built furniture for our front room out of old army surplus oak mess tables. Once when I was sick in bed for a couple of days, he taught me how to play chess, and we ate a whole box of Cheez-its together. And when our septic tank got full, he took care of that, too. He and I dug a big hole in a corner of the property, and then he climbed down in the septic tank. I couldn't believe he was going to do that. He'd fill up buckets with the sludge in the bottom of the tank, hand them up to me, and I'd put the bucket on a cart and wheel it over to the hole we'd just dug, empty the bucket and then go get another one.

Because the house was really small, he built an addition on it for our living room, and we turned the old living room into a bedroom. Like I said, it seemed to me that he could do anything. Once we were playing catch together and I decided to throw the baseball as hard as I could at him. He could catch anything I could throw at him. So I asked him if he'd ever thought about being a pro baseball player when he was younger. To my disbelief he told me that there was no way he could have been a professional—that he might seem good to me, but that those guys were really good. That was honestly hard for me to believe.

One Christmas, he made me a red and green tool

box, and inside were some tools just for me—a square, a coping saw, a screwdriver, a hammer, pliers and more. They each had their own position in the tool box. Really made me feel like I was a little man. Another Christmas, right after he'd finished the new living room, he bought Pat, Judy, and me each our own bb guns. Genuine Daisy single shot bb rifles. Undoubtedly from Sears. And he put a big target inside on the far wall of the new living room. By the end of the day, there were bb's embedded all over the new drywall in circles around the target. And Dad didn't even get mad. It's amazing none of us got seriously hurt those next few years, as Judy and I would use them constantly outside.

In the fourth grade, I had a teacher named Mrs. Rohrs. She'd been Pat's fourth grade teacher, too. We were each assigned a country on which to do a report. Mine was Colombia. I remember not knowing even how to begin, and Dad suggested that I write a letter to the president of Colombia, asking him the questions we were supposed to answer in the report. Sounded like a good idea to me, so I wrote a letter, and addressed the envelope to "The president of Colombia, Bogota, Colombia." Dad or Mom must have figured out how much postage it took. Time went by and I didn't hear anything, so managed to find out answers to almost everything by using the encyclopedias at the library. I hadn't known about encyclopedias earlier. We had to make a page showing the map of Colombia, and I couldn't find one, so I just made one up from my imagination, complete with mountains and rivers. I placed three or four cities in places where I thought they could possibly be. I got an A on the report and the teacher never said anything about the map.

About a month after the reports were due, I got a letter in the mail in Spanish, from Colombia. The stationery it was written on had *The President of Colombia* monogrammed at the top. It was really cool because it had stamps from Colombia on the envelope and I was a beginning stamp collector. The teacher in the room next door translated it, and it was quite the sensation. Mrs. Rohrs read it to the whole class. Once again, Dad had made me proud with his good idea.

Fourth grade was also the year I won the Park Lodge school spelling bee. Life's little victories. But I remember being a little hesitant to ask Mrs. Rohrs any questions— she seemed a bit disconnected from us — like not fully there. Mom explained to me that her husband was a soldier in the Korean War and that she was undoubtedly worried and distracted. I recall towards the end of that year, really having to need to go number one right before school got out. I must have been afraid to ask her, and I just tried to hold it, after all it was only ten more minutes. It really started to hurt, and fifteen seconds before the bell rung, I made a decision to let loose. Man! I had no idea how much there was going to be. It was running down my leg and everything, so when the bell rung, I bolted for the door and ran the mile home so no one would see me. Nobody did see me, but my leg was chafed and burning by the time I got home. Mom was very sympathetic about it and let me have a bath even though it wasn't Saturday night.

I discovered something along the way about moms and dads. At least for my growing up. I know you can't lump all dads and moms into the same mold. My Mom was the kind nurturer. Always there. She took care of keeping me and my clothes clean, she gave me medicine and care when I was sick, she comforted me when I got hurt, she made my lunches to take to school, etc. She was the steady Eddy. Or, in her case, the always there Olga. She was also the one who administered spankings when I deserved one. Dad didn't do a lot of that. I more remember him for the extra stuff. The outdoor projects, the fun stuff, playing catch, or fixing my bike, etc. Taking us fishing, teaching me chess. But I remember Mom for entirely other things.

I had hernia surgery in the third grade. It was Mom who brought me things to occupy my time while in the hospital. It was Mom who carried me from the car into the house when I got home. She was the one who asked me what I wanted for breakfast. She was the one who taught me how to make French toast, and tomato soup, and scrambled eggs, etc. She was my good friend, as well as my mom. Every fall, she'd take me to People's Store in Lakewood and I would get some new school clothes. I remember getting new shoes with her at our local shoe store when my old ones were worn out or didn't fit anymore. On one occasion the shoe salesman told me that with these new Keds, I could climb trees like a cat.

I was excited! Went home and tried to climb our biggest Douglas fir tree like a cat. Man, was I disappointed. Win a few, lose a few.

Both Mom and Dad could explain things well. At the start of fourth grade, I found myself flunking arithmetic for the first week or two. One morning at the breakfast table, I cried and told Mom I didn't want to go to school. When she asked why, I told her about my arithmetic problem, so she sat down with me and gave me some addition and subtraction to do. It turns out I was adding and subtracting starting with the left hand column, not the right. It was that simple. It turns out that I'd forgotten over the summer, and my teacher didn't catch why I was making the mistakes. I was incredibly relieved and gave Mom a big hug. That was only one of the many times she rescued me.

Our little brother, Steve, was born when I was in the second grade. We had a substitute teacher the day he was born, and the way I found out was that after lunch, the teacher announced to the class that Joey Kempston had a new baby brother. He turned out to be a beautiful little blonde guy who always smiled. So now we had six of us around the dinner table every night. Steve added a lot of enjoyment to all our lives.

Our house had an oil furnace which provided heat to a grate on our hall floor. That grate really got hot. In the winter, we'd often gather around it to put our clothes on because it would be pretty cold in our rooms. It felt so good to stand around that thing. Poor Steve fell on it once or twice and got little crisscross burn marks on his legs and arms.

Because Mom had a little one at home all day now, she made herself available to take care of two other toddlers who were Steve's age. One was Roger, the other was David Rowland. David's mother was the one who did Mom's hair. David and my brother, Steve, became good pals, and would push each other around the backyard in a broken down old baby carriage which had collapsed permanently. They loved it because it had wheels.

At the dinner table when we'd finished eating, one of us would read from Egermeier's Bible Story Book. There were questions at the end of each chapter, and we'd take turns answering them. The first years we lived in Tacoma we attended Ponder's Corner Church, a very small church on the old Highway 99. Church became fun in the fourth grade for me when we began attending Lake City Community Church. We'd go to church and Sunday school on Sunday mornings, and youth group and evening church on Sunday nights. I made good friends with the pastor's son, Mark Sweeney, and we did stuff together. I got to go to camp with Mark at Black Lake Bible Camp the summer after the fourth grade, and the following summer at Sammamish Bible Camp. The camp at Black Lake was primitive and had an outhouse in back of our dorm. At night before getting in our bunks, some of the boys would pee out the second story windows in order to avoid going outside to the outhouse in the dark. You can guess what I did.

One night after evening church, I went in my bedroom, entered the closet, shut the door, and told God that I would like to follow Him. Looking back, I had been a believer in God since I had first heard about Jesus, but I just wanted to make sure that He knew. I had an old Bible which had belonged to my Grandma Miller in its better days. It had a ripped leather cover, but it was mine and I liked it. The fact that Mom and Dad believed was good enough for me in those days when my knowledge was still pretty limited. I loved Mom and Dad and trusted them. They were intelligent people. Later I would make my faith my own. There was plenty of time for that down the road.

I was not always a good little kid. Once, Neal and Pete Dempsey took us with them to the newly vacated Italian diner up the street a few blocks. Amerigo's Restaurant had been shut down by the health department and was empty, but Neal knew how to get in through a back window. We looked in the main customer part of the restaurant and then entered the kitchen, where Pete took a billy club and ran it down the row of glasses knocking them all over on the floor. The sound was deafening and we all got scared and took off in a hurry.

The worst thing I ever did was break a bunch of windows in the back of Barr's warehouse. Their warehouse was just across the fence from our baseball field, and some windows were very close to first base. So if you fouled a line drive just outside of first base, it could break one of their windows. And that's exactly what occurred a couple of times. Mr. Barr happened to see us playing ball one time, and said that we shouldn't worry about the windows being broken because our field had been there before he built the warehouse. He was very nice. But apparently his niceness about the windows caused me to totally disrespect two or three panels of windows on the other side of the warehouse, nowhere near our field, because the day I discovered them, I broke a couple. Then I went back the next day and broke a few more, until all of them were broken. Looking back, I still can't believe I did that. Decades later, I did try to find Mr. Barr's son, Larry, to make amends, and to pay for the windows, but couldn't locate him.

From first through the fourth grades, I caught the school bus several blocks away. We'd always take the bus to school, but sometimes walk home if the sun was shining. My sister, Pat, became a patrol girl somewhere along the way, which meant you wore a badge and helped the school keep order. One time at the bus stop a kid started a fight with me. Not an uncommon thing. Most guys got in a little playground fight once a year or so with somebody. I never started one, but was not afraid to hit back. These were never huge things, and once you threw a kid down, the fight was usually over. Anyway, Pat flashed her badge to the kid and stepped in to stop the fight. I've always remembered that. It was nice of her. I was pretty sure he didn't know that the cop was my sister.

Behind the bus stop was a field with some hills on it, and that's where the whole neighborhood would go sledding whenever we had an inch or two of snow. That was really fun. Dad had told us about how fun it was to go tobogganing, but we had never seen one. So he built a toboggan out of those oak mess tables from Fort Lewis, but it never worked. He hadn't designed the runners very well. He would also pull us behind his car on our American Flier sleds. That was always fun. And illegal. We'd only do it on back roads.

Neal introduced Judy and me to golf. Meadow Park Golf Course was just a couple of miles away. We talked Dad into taking us down to Goodwill in Tacoma, and bought some clubs. Irons cost a dime each and woods were a quarter. The woods were old and beat up, but we shined them up with shoe polish. Meadow Park had a regular course plus another one called a short nine. The holes on the short nine course were from 90 to 180 yards long—just the perfect distance for us. We'd put the golf clubs across our handle bars, bike down there, and play quite often. When we'd run out of balls, we'd walk over to the back nine of the regular golf course, where two of the holes crossed a steep canyon with a creek down at the bottom. We'd make our way down that steep canyon-like hillside through a lot of nettles and blackberries and find golf balls, always watching out carefully for the course marshal because we weren't supposed to be down there. I got so excited about golf that I made a little miniature golf course in our back yard to practice putting.

In the summer time I'd bicycle down to our local library a lot. I'd read adventure books, westerns, and sports books by the dozen. One summer the library had a contest for who would read the most books over the summer. I didn't know about it, but Mom evidently did. She kept track of the books I read, and to my surprise, at the end of summer I won the contest which I didn't even know I had entered. It wasn't a big deal to me, but reading was sure a fun part of every summer. That's probably where it became a lifelong habit.

At five o'clock on weeknights, we'd gather around the radio in the living room and listen to radio programs. There were usually at least two half-hour programs. Sky King, Sergeant Preston of the Yukon, and The Green Hornet were my favorites. I remember sending fifty cents in to the sponsor of the Sky King program to buy a Sky King ring with a secret compartment. That was a disappointment and a waste of fifty cents. It wasn't a secret compartment at all; it was a very obvious compartment! Roy Rogers and Dale Evans had a western radio program. They always ended it with singing "Happy Trails to You," and then Roy would say, "And may the good Lord take a liking to you."

There was a family two blocks away who got the first tv in the neighborhood. Around 1950. We didn't know them, but Neal did and he invited us to come along with him a few times to watch Hopalong Cassidy on their brand new, modern, black and white 17-inch television. We even joined the "Hoppy" club.

Dogs were always a big part of our lives. I got my first dog bite from Rusty, Jimmy Moe's reddish cocker spaniel across the street. When we moved to the house on Steilacoom Blvd our dog, Sam, a good old American mutt, made the move with us. Sam had probably had distemper or something on the ranch in Oregon, because there he had what my parents called "fits." He would run in circles around the farmhouse five or six times, then stop out of exhaustion and lay down. He was over that by the time we moved to Tacoma. He loved to chase cars and it was one of those car chases which ended his life. After school one day, Mom told me she had some hard news to share. Sam had had his last car chase and it hadn't gone well. As they say, at least he died doing what he loved.

Next we had a beautiful female collie, Jill. In those days people didn't spay or neuter their pets much. So Jill got pregnant with half Collie-half Dalmatian pups. Rebel, down the street, JL's Dalmatian, obviously being the guilty party. The next time Jill went into heat, Dad spotted a beautiful big male collie hanging around—we never knew where he came from—and locked him in the garage with Jill for a couple of nights. He probably thought he'd died and gone to doggy heaven. Sure enough, down the line, Jill had beautiful Collie pups. We kept one of them, named him Jack, and he became our beloved dog for the next twelve years.

Nobody in the neighborhood had much money. Everybody drove older used cars and changed their own oil. Folks did their own repair work—plumbing, electrical etc. Both Dad and Mom took on extra jobs to make ends meet. Dad worked for a real estate lady on weekends repairing anything which needed repairing in her rental homes. Mom would babysit a lot, especially, it seemed to me, for USAF families whose husbands were often overseas during the Korean War. She'd make 35 cents an hour before midnight, and 50 cents an hour after. Pat and Judy would often get those jobs if Mom was busy.

Despite not having a lot of money, we did take mini-vacations in the summer time—once a year down to Grandpa and Grandma Kempston's house in Eugene, Oregon. That was cool because we'd pick strawberries and cherries and eat watermelon. Once Dad and I drove down together, just the two of us. I remember having lunch in a cafe with him. We literally never ate meals out, so that was a treat. I remember it was 240 miles to Eugene and Dad told me it was pretty good if you could average 40 miles per hour. So I watched the time closely and reported every hour how we were doing. We beat the average. We also took weekend trips about once a year to Benbow Lake Resort, Lake Kachess, or Sol Duc Hot Springs. Often on trips in those days, there would be car trouble - flat tires, overheating, or wheel bearings. All things which Dad could fix.

I liked school. In the fifth grade, I had Mrs. Justin as a teacher. Both Pat and Judy had been in her class during their 5th grade year. Starting with Mrs. Justin and lasting for another five years, I began to get marks on my report card essentially saying that they would like it if I could be a little less disruptive in class. I think technically it was something like "Needs to learn to work quietly without disturbing others." This was not something I was particularly aware of. I'd often finish in-class assignments early, and I had a sense of humor, and the combination of those two obviously didn't much add to class serenity.

One afternoon right after lunch in Mrs. Justin's class, I had said something which I thought was amusing to a friend. Mrs. Justin asked me to please step outside in the hallway for awhile. I was out there for a very long time. Two hours. Finally, school got out, and Mrs. Justin was saying goodbye to students from her doorway. She spotted me standing there outside the door: "Joey, I'm so sorry, I totally forgot you were out there!" I was actually glad not to get a lecture. I hadn't minded being out there at all.

In the spring of the fifth and sixth grades, Navy Base school held "field days," where you would compete against the entire school in different events. Judy really did well in these. Both years she won the girls' 50-yard dash, softball throw and high jump. She probably won the long jump, too. In those days the long jump was called the broad jump.

I must have been at least a little fast, because I came in third in the boys' 50-yard dash both years. As I said earlier, I had nowhere near Judy's athletic ability, but third wasn't all that bad. After we got our ribbons a couple of us guys were talking about it, probably a little proudly, and the two girls in our class, Donna and Dixie, who had come in first and second place for the girls in our grade, overheard us. They said they were probably as fast as we were. We said no way, and so they challenged us to a race at recess. They were two of the shortest girls in our class, but they beat us fairly. It's good to be humbled.

In the sixth grade, I was selected to be "Student of the Month" one time, and the school paper had an article on me. In the interview for the article they asked the usual questions—*What do you like to do in your free time? What is your favorite book? Who is your favorite movie star?* Etc. I had only been to a couple of movies in my whole life, so I said the only movie star's name I could recall, Betty Grable. Turns out that Betty had been last year's news about a decade prior. I took a little heat on that one as classmates chuckled when they read the article.

In the winter of sixth grade, it had rained a lot so we had to stay inside at recess more than usual. I taught a couple of guys how to play chess, and they taught a few more. So we ended up having a chess tournament in the class and I won. Hardly fair. Also that year, our teacher, Miss Baunsgard, would read us a story after lunch for a few minutes. Once when she was in the middle of reading "Around the World in Eighty Days" I was sitting next to Cathy Jacobs, a good friend. I was about to find out how good a friend she was.

Cathy's skirt was hiked up a bit above her knee, and I got this crazy notion to snap her leg with a rubber band which I always had a few of in my cigar box. In those days, kids always kept their crayons, pencil, paste, etc. in a cigar box in their desk. So I got one out, pulled it back and let her have it. I honestly didn't know how much it would hurt.

To say she screamed loudly was an understatement. Miss Baunsgard rushed over to her and said, "Cathy! What's the matter? What happened?" Oh, goodness, was I going to be in trouble! Cathy regained her composure and ever so calmly told her, while looking directly at me, that a bee had landed on her leg and she thought it was going to sting her. She said she was sorry for the disruption. I couldn't believe it. I silently mouthed "I love you" to her. She wrote something on a note and passed it to me. It said, "A friend in need is a friend indeed." Cathy moved away at the end of the year, but I've never forgotten her.

Mark Sweeney, the pastor's son, and I were asked to sing as a duet occasionally at Sunday night church, which was kind of an informal service. Mark and I both enjoyed it. We must have been halfway decent, because a lady in the congregation heard us sing and talked to my Mom about me taking voice lessons from her. Maybe Mom was feeling guilty because Pat had taken piano lessons and Judy, violin lessons, and I had never had musical lessons. So she agreed to the proposal. I wasn't real jazzed about it, but because I usually tried to honor Mom's desires, pretty soon I was taking voice lessons. My voice teacher discovered that my class at school was having a talent show, and somehow I got volunteered. So at our class's talent show in the 5th grade, I sang solo a cappella, *Great is Thy Faithfulness*. No big deal, but I remember being relieved when it was over. That solo was the only solo in my entire singing career.

Several decades later, I discovered where the lyrics

had originated. They were based on an encouraging scripture in Lamentations 3:22-23: "The steadfast love of the Lord never ceases, his mercies never come to an end; they are new every morning; Great is thy faithfulness."

His mercies. They are new every morning. Looking back at those six years on Steilacoom Boulevard I can see God's mercies and faithfulness at every turn. To begin with, He placed me in a family who demonstrated each day how kindness, honesty, hard work, and love made life work well. And through Judy, Neal and my pals He had shown me adventures, goodness, loyalty, and a whole lot of fun.

In the spring of 6th grade, we moved to a big, beautiful, old house on the other side of Lakewood, but I remain so grateful for the memories of being a kid in that little house.

CHAPTER 2
Joey in Junior High — The Good, The Bad, The Mischievous

I COULDN'T BELIEVE WHAT WAS happening. I was being directed to head down to the boiler room by my PE teacher, Mr. Gee. And he seemed way angrier than he should have been. After our showers in PE class that day, a friend and I were combing our hair in front of the locker room mirror. He splashed a little water on me with his comb and I retaliated in a friendly way. No big deal, but some water got onto the mirror. Mr. Gee walked by, noticed the water and demanded to know who had done it. We both admitted that we had. Evidently we'd pushed one of his buttons (who knew?) and we were led to the infamous boiler room by Mr. Gee, paddle in hand.

When we got there he said to me, "Son, take your glasses off, lean over and grab the staircase." I resented him calling me "son," ignored what he'd said about my glasses, leaned over and grabbed the staircase. He delivered three loud whacks to my rear end. It hurt like mad, but I didn't let on that I was even bothered. Junior high was like that for me. I got struck on the behind on three different occasions for extremely minor offenses.

Mr. Gee was involved with two of them. But I've gotten ahead of the story.

In April of 1953, at the tail end of my sixth grade year and right before entering junior high, our family made a move across town to a big old house on a hill in the middle of a forest of Douglas fir trees and rhododendrons. Everything changed dramatically. I loved the new place. For me it was like Narnia—completely magical. There was so much to explore and appreciate.

The house sat on four and a half acres and you couldn't see anyone else's house from ours. Incredible change from living on a busy boulevard. The house had not one, but two, fireplaces. We'd never had even one before. It had three bathrooms. We were used to just one for the six of us. The house had been built in 1909 and had two stories plus a walk-up attic, and half of a basement. When you walked out onto the back porch, there was a three-car detached garage with an old apartment above it, and a huge shed in back of that. The property even had a pump house over a well. And we had driveways leading to two different streets—Tower Road and Interlaaken Drive.

Dad had negotiated a real deal on the place. It had been owned by the Morrow family for many decades and Mrs. Morrow, then quite old, had been trying to sell it for some time. She was asking $30,000. Dad had been looking for a place like this for a few years, but couldn't afford that price. The real estate person told him to go ahead and make a low ball offer. That he did. Dad offered her $15,000 and she accepted it. Just like that we had our dream house.

Because the house and the property were both so large compared to where we'd lived before, I spent the first few days in the new place simply exploring. We discovered that it had a clothes chute from the second floor master bath down to a laundry room. So when you had dirty clothes, you just tossed them down the chute. In the master bedroom the closet went clear through to an adjacent room. You could actually go from one room to another that way. In the kitchen, which had the usual gas stove, there was also a wood burning stove with a dumbwaiter nearby to bring up wood from the basement. We got Dad to haul us up in it just for fun one time. In the attic we found an old wooden chest which looked like it came from an old sailing ship, and in the shed outside I discovered a large artillery shell casing from one of the World Wars.

I didn't think of this until decades later, but in moving we'd left behind some things which had been a huge part of our lives. The neighborhood gang of friends to play with was one. Here there simply wasn't one. That meant no baseball or football games after school. We didn't use our bikes anymore either. Lakewood junior high kids didn't seem to ride bikes much. And Judy and I had gotten too old for forts. But there were to be other things.

Work would be one of these and it started right away. A retired army colonel lived across the street and because his cook/cleaning lady knew Mom, I was recommended to do some yard work for him right off the bat. Col. McCook was very old, and seemed a tad stern to me, but I trekked on over and worked on his place one afternoon in June. I raked leaves, hauled and stacked firewood, swept walkways, and three hours later he gave me $3. That was an enormous amount for me. I remembered babysitting a few times in earlier years making thirty-five cents an hour. This was a buck an hour!

Well, I couldn't wait to share my good fortune with Dad, so I waited down in the driveway until he got home from work. When I told him I'd earned $3 he made the biggest deal out of it. "Wow, Joey! 3 bucks!" He said. "Do you think maybe if Mom and I end up a little short on money this weekend, we could borrow some of it for groceries?" I beamed: "Sure, Dad." He always did such a good job of making me feel like a man. That's one of those things a dad should be responsible for doing for his sons—and he modeled that well for me.

One of the first big jobs on the new home was to refurbish the decrepit apartment above the garage so we could rent it out. I took pride in being Dad's right hand man on that. Or, right hand pest, depending on the day. One day we were carrying pieces of heavy sheetrock two at a time up the steps to the apartment. Dad was on the front end and I was on the back end when he messed up and hit an overhead beam with the front of the sheetrock. It stopped dead in its tracks. I didn't, banging into the sheetrock full force with my face, breaking my glasses. I can still feel the pain in my schnoz.

We tiled the entire floor of the apartment with little square linoleum tiles and I got to help with that, too. Dad possessed a flair for design and we had fun with it. He and I talked about all kinds of things while working together. He wasn't particularly a talkative guy, but I was curious and asked a lot of questions and he had good answers. We ended up talking a lot — and I liked that. One Monday in July that summer we had some really good news to discuss and rejoice about. Ever since the fourth grade, I had been aware of and concerned about the Korean War. On this day in July an armistice had been declared. I remember being very glad it was over.

Uncle Carl, my Mom's little brother, had been a soldier when the Korean war broke out and my Dad interfered with his going to Korea, because Carl's brother, my Uncle Dick, had been killed in World War Two. Dick's death designated Carl as the member of a Gold Star family. When Carl was about to ship out to a combat zone in Korea, Dad actually went down to the station and got him off the train, explaining to his CO that he was from a Gold Star family and that the law prohibited him from duty in a combat zone. He may very well have saved Carl's life. Living close to McChord AFB and Fort Lewis, we had known a number of families who had lost loved ones in the war. I was really relieved that it was finally over—in the end, 36,000 US soldiers had died.

We finally finished the apartment overhaul and rented it out, furnished, for $65 a month. Dad and Mom had many soldiers' families and others in and out of that little apartment over the next few decades. We still remember the first renter. Dad nicknamed him "Little Zitzit" in honor (or dishonor) of the way he'd gun the engine in his car every morning. An army cook, Zitzit had to be at work way before the sun came up. It was winter and he'd start his car at four in the morning and let it warm up for 10 minutes, gunning the engine regularly. It drove both Mom and Dad nuts because it woke them up, every single morning. Zitzit also started a fire once by smoking near a gas can out in the driveway. He used to offer Mom free food from Fort Lewis, but she turned it down because it was stealing. Over the years, Zitzit was replaced by many others. Most of whom we really liked.

Joe and Tiny Hollis were some of those. Joe was a strapping soldier who was nineteen or twenty. Tiny was just fifteen and was indeed tiny. They were newlyweds from the southern backwoods. Soon after they moved in, Mom invited them over to have Sunday dinner with us. Joe wandered into the kitchen ahead of the meal commenting on the delicious aroma. Mom said it was a lamb roast and should really be tasty. Joe got this alarmed look on his face and whispered to us that Tiny didn't eat lamb. So we told him to tell Tiny it was pork roast. Fifteen minutes later we were all watching her out of the corners of our eyes as she bit into the lamb. Several minutes later she commented on how good the "pork roast" tasted. Smiles all around.

I made friends with a new kid that summer, Russell Sheiks. He was only in the area for a few months while staying with a cousin, but he was significant in my life. One afternoon we were together at a public swimming spot on American Lake when Russell found out I didn't know how to swim. He offered to teach me and had me lie flat and facedown in the water to show me that I could float. He called it the "dead man's float," and it worked. I found it surprisingly simple. Next he instructed me to kick with my feet and paddle with my hands and called it "dog paddling." So I followed his directions and that worked, too. I travelled a few yards and then did it again. Then he told me to pull my head out of the water while still lying flat and paddling. I looked at Russell and he gave me thumbs up and said, "Joey, you're swimming!"

That's where I got a little overconfident. A floating raft was offshore about twenty yards, so I headed for it, dog paddling the entire way. Try it sometime. It takes a long time to get anywhere when all you're doing is dog paddling. Halfway to the raft I was getting pretty tired and wondered if I could make it, but I kept going until I finally reached it. Wow. I had actually learned how to swim! Thank you, Russell. It was another of those proud moments a few hours later when I shared with Dad and Mom that I'd learned how to swim. Life's unexpected little triumphs.

That fall I started seventh grade at Hudtloff Junior High, a brand new school. We were the first students to ever set foot in the place. It even smelled clean and new. We had seven periods each day that year and an unpleasant thought soon hit me. I only used to have to convince one teacher that I was worthy of an A grade—now I have to convince a bunch.

I joined beginning band and chose the baritone horn to play without realizing it was the heaviest, largest instrument a kid could play that was required to be taken home every night. I hauled that thing on and off the bus almost every morning and afternoon until I got to high school. That first afternoon I sat in the living room on our piano bench trying to figure that baritone out. The problem was that you could hold any combination of the three valves up or down, or leave them all up, and you'd still blow different notes depending on how hard you puckered your lips. I didn't have a clue which note was which. Mom to the rescue. She heard me getting frustrated and had a great idea. "Let's hit "C" on the piano and match it up with the horn." Great idea, but it didn't work. It wouldn't match up. I found out the next day from my band teacher, Mr. Taylor, that the piano is a C instrument and the baritone is a B-flat instrument, so it never would have matched. Live and learn.

We had what they called a "core" class each day at school. The same teacher taught us for three periods a day and covered geography and social studies. My core teacher, Mr. McStott was brand new to the teaching profession, He'd recently been discharged from the Navy. I liked him and he liked me. I had him for math also. I remember being assigned to do a big report on the lumber industry in the Northwest. When I got it all done I showed it to Dad. He came up with a unique idea—since it was a report on lumber, how about using quarter inch mahogany plywood for the front and back covers. So I did that and used my wood burning set to write the title and my name. It came out really nice. For hinges on the report, Dad cut some old leather from his Sam Brown belt which had been part of his army uniform during the war. Mr. McStott liked it and gave me an A. I still have that report in a box somewhere.

I remember Valentine's day that year for a couple of reasons. Every year from first grade through the sixth, each kid in every class got a valentine from every other kid in the class. It had always been fun. You'd find out which girls liked you because a few of them would usually write gushy stuff. Not this year. I got zero valentines. I didn't like that. But I was intrigued by a contest which had been announced in the school newspaper around the valentine's theme. The object was to make as many words as possible from the letters found in "Valentine's Day." I worked on it in my spare time in class and at home over the weekend. I won the contest. The prize was no big deal, my choice of two books from the *Junior Scholastic* magazine—but the challenge it posed was fun.

In junior high, Judy and I didn't hang out together as much as we had before. We took a sabbatical from our "pal" relationship for a few years even though we still respected each other very much. Occasionally in school I would have the same teacher she'd had the year before—sometimes they were good and sometimes they weren't. Mr. Treloar was one of the good ones we both had, a wonderful man who made you feel good about yourself. He helped everybody, the not-so-good-students and the better ones alike. Mr. Stowe, another teacher we both had, was the opposite. He was a stubby little man with a pompous smirk who seemed to enjoy putting people down. He even required some of us to run for student body offices in an election, me included. When I told him I didn't want to, he said he would lower my grade. I should have told him "no" anyway, but didn't. So I ended up giving a speech in front of the whole student body. I lost to a good-looking girl named Judy whose speech was outstanding. She did a takeoff of the Gettysburg Address, but personalized it to fit her and Hudtloff Junior High. I was relieved not to win. I think I've always hated meetings and I would have had to go to a lot of them.

Two summers in a row Judy and I went on fun fishing trips with Dad, Grandpa Kempston, and Uncle Dave to Big Cultus Lake in Eastern Oregon. We took Uncle Dave's boat to an isolated part of the lake and camped there, just us. No one within miles. Every morning right after breakfast Dave and Grandpa would hike four miles in to Little Cultus Lake to fish. Judy and I would hike there later with Dad after we'd cleaned up from breakfast. On the way there, we were walking across a log over a creek, with Dad behind us. Suddenly we both turned around in alarm when we heard the log break behind us as Dad began walking on it. It toppled into the water, along with Dad, but he came out just fine, no injuries. That trip, Judy and I were both impressed because Dad did all the cooking. We didn't even know he could cook. The mosquitos on that four-mile hike were insatiable, but we made a game out of it, counting them as we sent them to mosquito heaven. And we nibbled on packs of Necco candy which Judy had brought along.

Back at home, I spent a lot more time alone in the Tower Road house than I ever had before, but it was good alone time. I worked a lot. Our brand new Sears lawn mower and I became good pals. We had a big lawn and I made it even bigger. I probably doubled the size of the lawn that first summer by carving out and taming new sections of very tall grass. Dad wasn't really good about keeping our gas can filled, so I'd get a little hose and suction gas out of a spare car we had, an old 1947 Studebaker. I'd stick one end of the hose down the gas tank of the Studebaker, bend down, making sure that I was lower than the gas tank, and suck on the other end for about two seconds before cramming it in the lawn mower's gas tank. I learned that if you sucked too long, you got a mouthful of gas, which I did about a third of the time.

After we finished the apartment overhaul, Dad got busy painting the old building which housed the garage, apartment, and shed. I usually took on most of the prep work, using a wire brush and scraper to get the old peeling paint off. I did a lot of that through the years. Another job I had involved the multiple dozens of sword ferns on the property. I'd use a big butcher knife to cut the old fronds off late in winter before the new fronds would poke themselves out to make the ferns look as good as they could. On one of my knife swings, my aim was off a bit and I opened up a large slice in my left thumb which bled like the proverbial stuck pig and throbbed for the rest of the day. Mom had to put three different bandages on it to quell the flow.

Looking back, I don't particularly remember Dad requiring me to help around the property. I pitched in because I knew it would help him. And he was always pleased with what I'd managed to get done. Not that he was excessive in his praise, because he wasn't. But I knew he was pleased and that made me feel good.

A tough thing happened to Dad when I was in the 8th grade. A tough thing which had a very good outcome—Romans 8:28 in action: "And we know that God causes everything to work together for the good of those who love him and are called according to his purpose for them."

Dad had worked at Fort Lewis for eight years as the civilian head of supply. And in these years, he always had a US Army counterpart—and boss—who held the rank of bird colonel. These guys would come and go every two years. Some of the rotating colonels were simply out for themselves and their army careers. In 1954 Dad got a particularly bad one who, after a few weeks, asked Dad why there were so many empty warehouses on north Fort Lewis. Dad replied that those were warehouses left over from World War Two and Korea, and that the fort had exactly the amount of supplies called for. The colonel told him to fill the warehouses up with cold weather gear, and Dad reiterated that they had precisely enough of every kind of equipment and supply which was needed for the amount of troops they had. The colonel, annoyed, said "Kempston, didn't you hear me? I want those empty warehouses filled with cold weather gear." Dad replied that he disagreed totally, but if the colonel insisted and would put it in writing, he would comply.

Months later, when the accountant from the Government Accounting Office came through to do the annual audit, he asked Dad why they had all this excessive cold weather gear stored on the post. They had way more than they were supposed to. Dad told him to see the colonel. Three minutes later the colonel came angrily out of his office, and in front of the government auditor, said, "Kempston, why do you have all this excessive gear stored on the fort?" To his credit, Dad told the colonel, in the words of the classic country song, "Take this job and shove it." He came home that night and told Mom that he had quit his job.

He was 45, had 4 kids, a wife, and a mortgage. Circumstances must have been difficult. But the atmosphere around the house didn't change. It remained a peaceful, kind, happy place. I'm sure that Mom and Dad had their moments in those months when he wasn't bringing home a paycheck, but I imagine they prayed and felt God's peace, not panic. After being out of work for several months, Dad was hired on at Fort Lewis by the Post Engineer's Department as the engineer in charge of the water supply, sewage system and garbage disposal. Because of the depression and World War Two, it had been 22 years since he'd gotten his degree in civil engineering but he finally had his first engineering job.

One of the benefits of Dad's new job for me involved fishing. On a couple of occasions Dad arranged for me to be dropped off at Lake Sequalitchew on Fort Lewis for a good part of the day. Sequalitchew was a spring-fed lake and the source of water for the whole fort. A big pumping station was the only thing on the lake and the pump station manager was a guy who Dad now supervised, Mr. Atwater. Mr. Atwater would take me out in a rowboat for two or three hours and we'd catch a string of rainbow trout. And that night Mom would cook them for dinner.

Dad always had a bit of the farm boy in him. He'd lived in the panhandle of Idaho on a farm as a kid for three years. Those years were by far his favorite part of growing up. He even rode a horse to school three miles every day. The reason I'm bringing this up is that Dad got the idea that we should have our own chickens for laying eggs. He'd bought a bunch of used screen doors from Fort Lewis for practically nothing, and constructed the chicken coop with them. He then bought a dozen laying hens. I was the designated chicken guy. Even though we all gathered eggs, it was my job to feed them, give them clean water, and clean their coop. I remember dreading going out there during the rainy winter giving them water and chicken feed and getting soaked in the process. The day that Dad decided to call this experiment to a halt was a happy day for me. I was more than eager to put their heads on the chopping block.

We really enjoyed our new home. Dad had given the exterior of the house a fresh coat of white paint complete with green window trim. He'd wallpapered a lot of the rooms. It really felt homey. We often enjoyed fires in the huge living room fireplace. One time Dad had burned a bunch of wadded up newspapers in the fireplace for some reason or other, and the inside of the soot-covered chimney caught fire. There were flames shooting out the top of the chimney. Fortunately for us it was a rainy day and nothing else caught fire. After that he made sure to clean the flue every few years by getting on the roof, lowering some chains on the inside of the chimney and banging them against the sides. We never used the fireplace in the den because Dad said it was too old, but we sure enjoyed the other one.

In the evenings Dad would often make popcorn in a pan on the stove and bring bowls of it in to whomever was in the living room. We got our first television when I was in the eighth grade. He and Mom had gone to an auction which they frequented, and bought a non-working set for $35, which he then fixed. He got an old antenna from the garbage dump at Fort Lewis, and our family entered the television era. I remember watching Lawrence Welk together as a family on Saturday nights with a fire going. My favorite program was "Navy Log," a half-hour program on Tuesday nights about the US Navy during World War Two.

Twice one summer in my junior high years a family friend, Larry, invited me along on an adventure with him to the Yakima area. Larry owned a local wrecking yard. He'd hitch a trailer behind his truck and head across the mountains with the purpose in mind of buying a couple of old horse-drawn wooden wagons from folks on the Indian reservations around Yakima and hauling them home. The two of us would stop at a roadside stand once we got closer to Yakima and buy a watermelon for three cents a pound, cut it in two and we'd each eat a half. In the summer heat it was absolutely delicious.

We'd camp somewhere in the hills outside of White Swan, which is in the middle of nowhere, and try to find some wagons to buy the next morning. In the early evening we'd hunt jackrabbits with twenty-two caliber rifles. Larry had one for each of us. This was the first time I'd ever shot a gun—I knew virtually nothing about guns except my own Daisy single-shot BB gun, which certainly didn't qualify as a "real" gun. I was standing to the left of Larry when he squeezed off his first shot. The noise was incredibly loud to begin with and when Larry's rifle automatically ejected the red hot shell casing, it landed on my neck and went down my tee shirt. I thought I'd been shot. I did the fanciest dance steps you ever saw trying to get that hot shell casing out of my shirt. Larry laughed till the cows came home—so much for me and guns.

Because we had so many Douglas firs on our property, every once in a while Dad would spot one which needed to be taken down because it was dead and probably dangerous. So my Uncle Harlow, who lived in Port Orchard about 45 minutes away, would bring his big chainsaw down and cut down the suspect tree. He'd been a logger before his career as a Navy chaplain. This was always exciting to watch. The aftermath was that I would have a lot of cut up logs to split for firewood. I spent more time than I ever wanted to with a sledge hammer and wedges, but we always had a good supply of firewood. We burned it in the kitchen wood stove as well as the living room fireplace.

One of the things we'd found on the property when we moved in was a one-man crosscut saw with a comfortable wooden handle on one end. It was probably between four and five feet long. One night in a storm the wind toppled a huge Douglas fir. The downed tree had a diameter of close to four feet and blocked the path that we used to get down to Tower Road to catch the school bus in the morning. I spent quite a few hours that next week sawing through the tree twice to provide a walkway through the log. I still have a scar on my knee from pulling the saw across it accidentally.

Later on I made a third cut through that tree in order to make a four-inch thick slab. I varnished one side of the slab and put dates on the different rings of the tree. The tree was over 200 years old, so I marked on one of the rings "1776" for when the US declared independence from England; another ring I marked with an "1865" for the end of the Civil War, etc. I took it to school and did an oral report on it for Mr. Herron's core class. Mr. Herron was one of my favorite teachers. He fought in World War Two in the Pacific as a marine on the island of Iwo Jima and several other islands. That's probably where he'd gotten his premature gray hair. He was a very kind man. My sister, Pat, had also had him for a teacher.

My brother, Steve, and I shared a bedroom at the end of the upstairs hallway. Despite, or maybe because of our age difference of seven years, we got along very well. I don't recall even one fight. He was really a good kid. Steve loved our new home. He and his buddy, David, even had their own "climbing tree," so named because the two of them spent many happy hours sitting up towards the top of it. It was a 50-foot high Hemlock. Dad found an old Briggs and Stratton lawn mower engine somewhere and built a go cart for Steve. Steve would drive lap after lap around our circular driveway in that thing.

My sister, Pat—four years ahead of me—went off to college after a couple of years in the new house. It was a sad day for all of us when she boarded the train at Union Station in Tacoma for Chicago. After she left, Dad had a hard time getting through his prayer before our dinner each night as he'd mention her name. We all really missed her. I don't think she ever knew how much.

School remained enjoyable for me in my junior high years. I liked the traditional subjects, but classes like band, shop (we had wood shop, radio shop, air shop) and PE added good variety. During the eighth and ninth grades, even though I continued to get good grades, I got in trouble every once in a while. Never for anything big, but definitely for something. My personal observation of those years were that some teachers really were positive and great encouragers, while others had the opposite effect and perhaps should never have been teachers.

I had Mr. Nojd for health. He was a teacher who enjoyed having the upper hand, and to me it seemed like an open invitation to irritate him. Both my sisters had been in his classes before as well. Pat had been an exemplary student, Judy gave him a bit of a hard time with her kidding, but I was merciless. One day he caught me staring out the window, which I was doing just to bug him, and he called me out on it—wanted to know what was so interesting out there. I told him I was just watching the birds. I kept it up from time to time just to be a jerk. I put a dedication page in my health notebook, dedicating it to "the birds outside Mr. Nojd's window." He was a chain smoker and all of his clothes reeked of smoke. In the notebook there was a section on the harmful effects of smoking and I personalized that for him, adding several lines like "Mr. Nojd—now is a good time to quit!"

We had good grooming contests in Mr. Nojd's health class every other week. Once he noticed me running a comb through my hair right before it was my turn to be inspected, so he had me stand in the corner and comb my hair for the rest of the period. Every time he'd turn his back toward the class I pretended to comb the hair under my arm and a few other places. Kids were laughing and he'd turn around to see what was going on. One time he'd had enough of my smart comments and took me to the boiler room and I got three strokes of his paddle. That was well-deserved.

To Mr. Nojd's misfortune, he also happened to be the bus driver on the route I took home. I walked home in nice weather but took his bus when weather was lousy. Sometimes I used to whack the stop sign which bus drivers would extend when the door was open to stop traffic. Well, one day Mr. Nojd was watching for me to whack it. He'd pulled the sign back a bit, waited for me to get in range, and then opened it very fast, slamming me in the face and knocking my glasses off. I think it was a harder hit than he'd intended. He hopped right off the bus and hurried around to ask if I was okay. I grinned and said I was.

But then I took the friendly battle with Mr. Nojd a little far. When I'd walk home his bus would pass me and then go slowly around a curve. I'd hold my fist up and as soon as he was around the curve, I'd give the bus the middle finger salute. My timing must have been a little off one day, because the next morning, he walked into my first period class before it started, grabbed me and said very calmly and firmly "I knew you'd mess up, Kempston, and I'd catch you sooner or later. I saw what you did yesterday and if you ever do that again, I'll break that finger off and stuff it up your nose." At that, he turned and walked away. It seemed the proper time to cease and desist. We'd actually grown to like each other. At least a little. And I did get an A in his class.

I took art from Mr. Thorpe. He was also a veteran of World War Two, having served in the Ninth Army Air Force in England. One day he told us that we could tell jokes for the last five minutes of class that day. I told one about three rabbits who were trying to swim across the Atlantic. The first rabbit ate carrots and made it halfway across. The second rabbit ate lettuce and made it two thirds of the way. The third rabbit was smarter than the first two. He ate beans and went putt-putt-putt all the way across. My joke got laughs, but Mr. Thorpe made me write a five hundred word essay on why you shouldn't tell off-color jokes in class. I opened the essay with something like, "You shouldn't tell off-color jokes in class. That is not good. Here are the kinds of jokes you should tell." And then I told jokes for another five hundred words. He liked it.

Mr. Blanchard was the mechanical drawing teacher. You could sometimes smell alcohol on his breath after lunch. I got into trouble talking in his class also, and was assigned to write a 1500 word original story. I remember writing it on our front porch one Saturday afternoon. I wrote a classic western story of a teenage boy from the western plains who left home, got a job as a ranch hand in another state and returned home three years later having grown into a man. Mr. Blanchard asked me to read it to the class, which I did. I thought it was a pretty good story.

Another day in his class did not turn out very well for me. A girl in our grade who we all knew walked into our classroom of all guys in the middle of the period to deliver a message to Mr. Blanchard from the office. Most of us knew her pretty well — she was engaging and fun. We were all busy working on our drawings until someone said hi to her. She said hi back, and pretty soon a couple of other guys said something to her, and then comments were just flying around the room. Everybody said something — nothing out of line — but the class did get a little out of control. I think most of us thought it was just a fun interlude in the day which he seemed to allow. After she left, we found out Mr. Blanchard didn't view it that way at all. He said that he was going to go up and down each row and you were to confess whether or not you had said anything. Because I was in the first seat on the left, I was the very first to be questioned. I was honest and said that I had said something even though I had really been relatively quiet. The guy behind me, Scott, admitted that he had said something also, but from then on as he continued up and down the rows, everyone lied. I couldn't believe it. A guy named Rich had been one of the loudest and when he denied any involvement, I whispered to him, "C'mon Rich, you were in on it big time." He whispered back that he was running for office and lied because he couldn't get in trouble. Typical politician.

This event happened on a Friday and we all thought it was all over. Not so. When class started on Monday, Mr. Blanchard sent Scott and me down to see Mr. Lang, our vice principal. Mr. Gee, the PE teacher who'd given me the paddle a week previous for the overblown water-on-the-mirror incident, happened to walk by and saw us sitting in his office. He came in and told Mr. Lang that I had been in trouble in his class recently and that both of us should really be taught a lesson. So we each got six swats with the paddle in the boiler room instead of the usual three. Three honestly hurt really badly, but the pain from six was incredible. I went first and didn't utter a sound although I was really hurting. Scott was next and after three, he asked if he could please have the other three later. Request denied.

On the way back to class my behind was so burning hot that I seriously considered going in the boys' lavatory, filling up the sink with some cold water, and dipping my behind in it to cool it down. Two days later it was still really sore, so I got a mirror to look at my derriere. I saw why it was so sore. It was black and blue. Mr. Gee remained my most unfavorite teacher and with good reason. That quarter my grades were all A's except for a D in PE from him—the only D I ever received.

An interesting side note—40 years later Cherry and I went to my 35th high school reunion. It was the first reunion I had gone to and the two of us had a great time. And I reconciled with Mr. Gee, although he had no clue. We were almost last in line getting our food so finding a table with any room left was difficult. Cherry finally found a table which had a couple of empty spots, but guess who was sitting there? Yes; Mr. Gee and his wife. I told Cherry there's no way we're sitting with him. Let's keep looking. But there was honestly no place else to sit. So we sat with him, I introduced myself and we had a good chat over dinner. Of course, he didn't remember me because I was at the front end of his thirty-five year teaching career. We had a very good chat. The lesson in this? It's never too late to forgive. And forgiveness is a very good thing. (Also, never be party to hitting someone until they're black and blue.)

I never told Mom or Dad about any of the trouble I had gotten into. But when the pain from the six swats lingered on, I did wonder for a few hours one night whether or not I was a bad person. I thought it over and concluded that I was not — at least most of the time. At least I'd been honest. That was not a fun incident. But I continued to like school.

Girls, I always liked them. There would usually be one I'd kind of like, but in junior high I never acted on it, and they never knew. I remember one morning on the school bus a neat thing happened. I had noticed a real cute girl who'd get on the bus the stop after ours. Janet was her name. She was always smiling, and wore a pink and black scarf over her collar. She was a grade younger than me. One morning I looked at her out the bus window and read her lips. She was telling her friend that she liked me and pointed to me. That made me smile on the inside. Oh, the little things we remember.

Summers were fun at the house on Tower Road. We had two apple trees, a cherry tree, a pear tree, and a whole bunch of blackberries. One of my favorite things to do on a sunny day was to sit in a comfortable spot in one of the apple trees and read. I'd bury my head in a book and eat a few apples. I'd even take a pillow up there to make it more comfortable. Mom made blackberry jam and canned cherries, pears and applesauce (plus a bunch of other stuff), but I never had to help with the canning. My sisters did. I would help pick the blackberries and the apples, but I've got fond memories of being up in that tree when the women were in the house canning. I didn't help much with housework; only when asked. Except for helping wash or dry dishes. I did the outdoor jobs and had weekly lawn jobs in the neighborhood. These extended into my high school years as well.

Another part of early summers in that house was daily vacation Bible school at Lake City Community Church. I attended for a few years, and then helped out for a few more. It was the week after regular school got out and it was always fun. I still can quote from memory the Bible verses we were encouraged to learn. I have found these words from Jesus in Matthew 11:28-29 to be so true my entire life: "Come to me, all you who are weary and burdened and I will give you rest. Take my yoke upon you and learn from me, for I am gentle and humble in heart and you will find rest for your souls. For my yoke is easy and my burden is light." That is just one of the many verses they had us memorize.

One of the things I loved to do in the summertime was visit the public swimming spot on American Lake when it was warm out. My friends and I would swim out to the raft and just lie there, soaking up the sun. When we got too hot, we'd just jump in for a bit, then climb back up. We enjoyed doing cannonball competitions off the raft. I had a friend named Tim McKernan, who occasionally would want to swim across the lake, so I accompanied him on an inner tube. It was about a mile across. I always wondered what would happen if the inner tube developed a leak when I was out there. I wasn't completely sure I could make it all the way back to the shore. Fortunately, I never got the chance to find out. Later on, I would practice swimming across nearby Steilacoom Lake which was only a half mile across.

At this stage of my life I began to notice that my parents were very giving people. They gave to people in all kinds of ways. Mom taught seventh grade Sunday school all through my junior high years. Dad was one of our church's trustees. He also painted the three church buses, with assistance from Judy and me. And he worked on the new sanctuary building under construction. I'd work with him on many Saturdays as the men in the church put up that building. Mom and Dad taught hospitality by example. For three months one year, a missionary couple from Ethiopia lived with us on their sabbatical. Mom and Dad invited people over for Sunday dinners often. These were sometimes single people, sometimes couples— military couples whom they'd met at church, or who lived in our apartment. They also opened up our home to foster care, and one year we took in several kids. Grandma Miller, Mom's mother, would also come once a year and stay for a few months. Both Dad and Mom looked after older women who needed help with finances, doctor visits, home repair, etc. Mrs. French and Miss Langworthy were two of those women. Proverbs 11:25 says something which described my parents: "A generous person will prosper; whoever refreshes others will be refreshed."

Mom continued to be such a good friend and mother. I continued to get new clothes once a year, right before school started. She'd take me down to People's Store near Lakewood Center and I'd get a new pair of pants or two, and maybe a couple of shirts. She was always the one who would take us to the doctor or dentist. I broke my glasses more than anyone I knew. New lenses were $3.30 each, and she bought me plenty of those through the years. She also attended every one of my band concerts, and baritone horn solo contests, which started in junior high and went all the way through my senior year. Another thing I particularly enjoyed were the few moments after I got home from school every day. I'd always eat something, and the two of us would sit in the kitchen and talk. She liked to be with me and I knew that. Before we would leave for school each morning, Mom would grab a verse of scripture from a little breadbox kind of thing and one of us would read it. That small act and many others made me realize that Mom and Dad really trusted God with every part of their daily lives.

Earlier I mentioned that I didn't ride the old bike much anymore. However, every once in a while Mom would ask me to pedal down to Lakewood Lockers to pick up some groceries she needed. In the 1950's there used to be small "mom and pop" style grocery stores with freezer lockers as a part of what they offered as a service to the public. Household refrigerators didn't have freezer compartments yet, so you could freeze meat, fish, or whatever you wanted to freeze at one of these kinds of lockers.

Lakewood Lockers was a half mile away out our back driveway. Halfway through my bicycle ride to the lockers I'd always encounter these two aggressive Basset hounds. They'd tear out of their yard onto the road barking like crazy and try to bite my ankles. One day I'd had enough even though I've always been a dog lover. These guys were particularly tenacious that day and so on my trip back from the store, I picked up two very large rocks and waited for the attack. Sure enough, they came. I waited until they were right beside me and let loose with both rocks one after the other. The rocks hit both of them on their heads, and as I bicycled off, they'd rolled over and were doing the Basset hound version of the rebel yell. They always left me alone after that.

A guy named Paul became one of my good friends. He was a grade ahead of me. We met at church and we both played in the band, so we had those two things in common. Paul's dad dropped him off at school on his way to work, so he began dropping by my house to pick me up also. That was kind of him. Paul was really good at music and with anything scientific. He knew how to explode things and was an interesting guy to be around. He tended to be shy and introverted, but he enjoyed my company and I enjoyed his.

Another friend was Rick. He was our pastor's son. Rick was two grades below me and was always doing questionable things, but he was fun to be around. Sometimes after church on Sunday mornings, his dad and mom would invite me along with their family to go out to eat at a restaurant on the waterfront in Tacoma called "Top of the Ocean." My family never went out to eat, so this was a treat. Rick and I would sometimes sleep over at each other's houses. We'd swim together at American Lake. He had a great treehouse in his backyard and we did a lot of stuff together. One summer night he showed up at our place with something kind of big and heavy in a paper bag. He'd gone through the old settlers' cemetery and stolen a gravestone to show it to me—like I wanted some old stolen gravestone. That was why we called him "Crazy Rick."

In the ninth grade, different shop classes were offered each quarter. In winter quarter I had radio shop from Mr. Erickson. The class was fun because he was fun. He was a ham radio enthusiast and told us that the class would essentially teach us how to get our novice ham radio license. Then he added the kicker. "If you pass the test for your novice license, and I'd be happy to give you the test, you get an automatic A in the class." So we learned basic radio theory and the Morse code. I took the test, passed it, and got my novice license. The novice license was only good for one year, and when you were on the radio, you were only allowed to communicate through Morse code.

Dad was very cool and took me down to C & G Radio in Tacoma and bought me a used already-assembled

Heathkit AR2 Receiver and an AT1 Transmitter. The receiver was $20 and the transmitter was $25. He helped me put a big long dipole antenna up outside my bedroom, and I went on the air. I wasn't expecting any of this. My call letters were WN7COF, or as Dad said, *WN7 Crazy Old Fox*. It took me a couple of afternoons calling "CQ" (meaning I would like to talk with anyone) from WN7COF, and I finally heard someone answering me back, in code, of course. I was very nervous but it worked, and I could read his code! It was a big thrill. It was some novice from Oregon. So I did ham radio for a good part of the rest of that spring and summer. It sounds dull and boring in these days of cell phones, texting, and emails, but at the time it was incredible to be able to talk with someone in another part of the country from my bedroom—it seemed like magic. And in a few days after a conversation with some other ham, you'd get a QSL card in the mail, verifying the radio contact.

So I ended junior high having learned about work, about the value of alone time, about having fun, about the consequences of wrong behavior and a slug of other things. High school was just around the corner and I was looking forward to it.

CHAPTER 3
Clover Park Where Days are Brightest . . .

WORDS SOMETIMES CHANGE THEIR meaning with the passage of time. When I entered Clover Park High School as a 14-year-old sophomore in September 1956, I discovered that after every home game the student body would stand together and sing the alma mater—the first few lines of which went like this:

> *Clover Park, where days are brightest,*
> *Clover Park, where friends are gay,*
> *On our field, a shield of valor,*
> *First in work and first in play.*

As I write this 63 years later, I'm betting they don't sing it anymore. Or, if they do, they've changed the words on line two.

Clover Park was a three-year high school. My fifth period class that sophomore year was beginning Spanish. Very soon it became by far my favorite class, the one I always looked forward to the most. Not because I loved "El Español," or the teacher, but because I sat between three of the cutest girls in the senior class. They liked me and I became their friend right off the bat. I never figured that one out exactly. They'd each needed an easy class as a senior, so they'd all elected to take beginning Spanish. It was absolutely beyond cool for me, a lowly sophomore, to sit between these fun senior girls, be included in their chit chat and have them smile and say "Hi, Jose," when I'd run across them in the hallways. Makes me smile even to remember it today.

A month before my sophomore year started, my appreciation for girls had hit an all-time high. A girl named Nancy had moved to Lakewood from Portland that summer. She was two grades below me in school—tall, blonde, and seriously beautiful with an engaging smile. I'd met her on a church youth group outing to Mount Rainier, and we'd managed to get in the same car for the ride home. By the time I was dropped off at my house, I knew that she liked me. My friend, Paul, told me that I could invite her to go with us in his car to "YFC" the next Saturday night. YFC was a large youth rally held at a church in downtown Tacoma every Saturday night. I'd often gone to it. On the way home that night sitting in the backseat of Paul's Dad's '56 Plymouth I held hands with a girl for the first time. Couldn't believe my good fortune. And we even kissed a few weeks later. Same backseat. Thank you, Paul.

Having Nancy for a girlfriend was just one of the things I liked about being a sophomore in high school. I liked being in the band. Half the starters on the varsity football team were in the band including the quarterback, fullback, and halfback. They played the clarinet, the trombone, and the oboe. Band was first period and that fall, as every fall, we'd spend three or four class times each week on the football field practicing formations and marching for the Friday night games. That fall our team won our league, which made us eligible to play the winner of the Seattle league on Thanksgiving morning, the Ballard Beavers, at Memorial Stadium in Seattle.

I remember two things about the game. Before kickoff, both bands assembled on the field to play the Star Spangled Banner together. Right off the bat, the director from Ballard was signaling something very vehemently to part of the band, but I honestly couldn't tell what he was trying to communicate. He looked chagrined and irritated with some embarrassment tossed in. As it turns out, the Ballard band was playing in the key of C and our band was playing in the key of B flat. I was in the middle of our band and couldn't hear anything except my instrument and the instruments around me. As it turns out, he was trying to signal to his own band to quit playing. Mom was listening to the game at home on the radio and said the dissonance was both painful and humorous to listen to at the same time. The band directors obviously hadn't thought to communicate with each other about the key. The other memorable thing about the game was that we were beaten very badly. In fact, our fullback and quarterback both got bones broken in the first half.

I never met with a school counselor while at Clover Park. I probably should have, because I had picked up the erroneous idea that you were required to take study hall each semester. I don't know how I got the notion, but scheduling study hall my first year and a half kept me from having enough room in my schedule for any science except physics. I also had no room for a second year of a language. Study hall met in a long, sloping classroom right next to the library. Anyway, I did use the time to do homework and eventually wised up and didn't take study hall anymore.

I was also a day late and a dollar short when it came to clothing styles. The first day in study hall my sophomore year I noticed a guy across the aisle wearing pants with a little belt buckle up high in back above the pockets. Why in the world would anybody have a belt buckle in the back of their pants? Weird. Pretty soon I noticed another guy wearing them, then another. It turned out they were all over the place. They were called "Ivy League pants" and they were *the thing* to wear. I had managed to miss the pink and black style which hit the scene in my junior high years as rock 'n roll exploded, but I was darned if I was going to miss the show this time. I wanted a pair! It took me only a few months to get them, but when I did, I got two pairs and they were free.

One of my regular lawn mowing jobs was for a guy who was a manager for the Day Pants Company in Tacoma. My first morning at their home was memorable. He took me to the garage and started explaining his lawn mower to me, not realizing that I had spent hundreds of hours behind all kinds of lawn mowers in the past three years. That's how I earned money. After he started the engine, he warned me loudly that mowers were dangerous and

I should always be careful and never put my fingers in the area where the blades were going around. Then he demonstrated where I shouldn't put my fingers, and he stuck one of his own right in the blades and cut the end of his finger off. Long story short, I mowed their lawn for three years, but never saw him again—I always dealt with his very nice wife. And on my birthday that first year, she asked me what size pants I wore, and got me two pairs of those cool Ivy League pants for free from her husband who was now sporting a shortened middle finger on his right hand. Probably made him think twice about flipping anyone off after that.

I mowed lawns regularly for a variety of people. The only job I was ever fired from was one of those lawn mowing jobs. I worked just a few times for a wealthy man who lived in a spacious estate on Gravelly Lake. He was stern-faced and made me feel uncomfortable—I didn't like working for him. The lawn was so big that it required a sit-down lawn mower, which he had. One day as he was driving his Lincoln Continental into the driveway, I was finishing a U-turn in front of his garage with the mower. I hadn't estimated the turning radius of the mower correctly and the right handlebar left a small scrape mark on his wooden garage door. He motioned me over and politely told me that he wouldn't require my services anymore and that I could go home. Walking home, I felt relieved.

Unlike how I felt in junior high, I liked all of my teachers in high school. Wally Erwin was the PE teacher. He graded his classes strictly on improvement in physical fitness, and gave us objective goals for pushups, sit-ups, pull-ups, etc. I did well in his class and learned the value of discipline from him. Everybody's favorite teacher was a young newhistory teacher recently discharged from the navy, Jerry Storvick. At class reunions years later, Jerry would come, remember our names, and tell stories about us. We'd quickly understand all over again why he was our favorite. He asked you questions outside of class when he'd bump into you. He'd compliment choir people on their songs and band kids on their performances at assemblies. I wrote my only term paper in high school for him on the battle for Iwo Jima during World War Two. He was kind enough to write a recommendation for one of my two college applications when I was a senior. Jerry Storvick was an example of how to be genuinely interested in other people and how to show it.

Renwick Taylor was our band instructor. I'd known him since the 7th grade. He'd been my beginning band instructor. I liked him and he liked me. He was personal and engaging—strict, but fun. One day he passed out music for a piece and told us to practice it and we'd try it all together in a week or so. I honestly doubt that any of us practiced it, because once we hit high school very few of us took our horns home anymore at night to practice. The baritone part was particularly difficult as we discovered when we tried playing the piece as a band the next week. We three baritone players massacred our part, so he had us try it alone without the rest of the band. That was worse. He let us know he wasn't happy about it, and moved on. After school I didn't want to take my horn home, but I knew I needed to learn the music. So I went in to one of the practice rooms and played it over and over again until I had it down. It took about forty-five minutes. It was difficult. Mr. Taylor happened to come in the room once, gave me a pleasing nod, and then walked out.

The next morning he began class with these words: "I want to share with you what I saw and heard in here yesterday after school. It was an example of diligence, an example of what we should all strive to be like. As you remember, the baritones sounded painfully bad yesterday morning on that new piece. You all were here and heard. Last night after school, I heard a baritone player practicing that part for a little under an hour until he learned it. That person was Joe Kempston. He is someone who strives for excellence." The class spontaneously clapped. My buddies around me smiled and quietly booed in a friendly way. It felt good.

When I was a senior I took a required class called Current Events from Bob Peterson, a tall, gangly teacher who always smiled. He was a happy, kind man—an encourager. I have a couple of memories from that class. One was when I was giving an oral book report on a World War One German ace pilot. Charlie Bergeron was sitting in the front row making faces at me. I had met Charlie in kindergarten a dozen years earlier, and he was now our senior class president and the best basketball player on our team. Charlie started me laughing and I couldn't stop. I finally had to sit down, report unfinished.

The other memory is not one to be proud of particularly, but it was funny. The second week of the semester Mr. Peterson assigned each of us a TV program to watch every week. Each program related to current happenings in the world. Mine was called something like *Weekly News Summary*, and was broadcast Saturday nights at ten p.m.. He said to watch our designated program as often as we could, and sometime later in the semester he would give us a pop quiz on it. The quiz would constitute twenty-five percent of our grade for the semester.

I was usually out on Saturday nights, but even on the nights I was home, I'd forget to watch it. One Friday in December, the inevitable finally came. Mr. Peterson told us to pull out some paper and write a few pages about what we'd learned from our particular program. He told us to be very specific. I sighed and whispered to my buddies within hearing distance that I was in trouble because I hadn't watched it once. I then wrote two pages of very specific unadulterated fantasy on what I'd "learned." Before passing out the graded papers the following Monday, Mr. Peterson said that most of the papers were good, but that there was one paper that was particularly outstanding and that he wanted the whole class to hear it. He walked over to me, handed me my paper, and asked me to read it aloud. I looked at the grade he'd given me—an A+. I then read it aloud, again to quiet boos from my friends. At our 50th class reunion, I shared the story with him, and we both laughed. He complimented me on my ingenuity.

Leota Lackey was the teacher who taught all the advanced math classes. I had her as a teacher my last two years. She was a bit older, and didn't put up with any nonsense, but had a wry smile and a twinkle in her eye. About a month before we graduated, Mrs. Lackey offered to sell to anyone who wanted it a review book which would cover all of geometry, trigonometry, advanced algebra, and precalculus. She told us if we were going to major in engineering or the sciences in college that we should begin working our way through the book in August before we headed off to our various colleges. She said it would be a great recap to refresh us as we took college math placement tests. I took her advice, and it worked! I was able to skip a couple of college math classes as a result. Thank you, Mrs. Lackey. She was definitely another teacher who taught me about diligence.

I had a routine with my studying. If I couldn't get it all done in study hall, which I usually couldn't, I'd do my school work in my room as soon as I got home, simply to get it over with. Sometimes, as math became more complicated, I'd ask Dad for help when I just couldn't solve a problem. I was always amazed that he'd sit down with me, review the book a little, and recall his math from 25 years ago at the University of Illinois.

I still spent a lot of time in my high school years working with Dad. One evening after dinner on a school night, he asked me to help him paint his office at Fort Lewis. It was a large area with multiple desks. He estimated that we'd be done late, maybe even as late as midnight. We had a good time painting and talking together. Midnight rolled around and we weren't close to being done. Finally around two a.m. we were almost done, when Dad accidentally knocked a gallon of paint off his ladder. We looked at each other and started to laugh, because that mistake had just added another 20 minutes of clean-up time to the job. Then I made him laugh even harder when I told him that he probably wouldn't be laughing if I had been the one who'd spilled the paint bucket. We ended up getting home around three a.m. That was really special. I loved being with him.

In my junior year, Dad decided to build a rental cabin on the property to help with the expense of Judy and me being in college at the same time in two years. Our property had plenty of room, so he picked a site that couldn't be seen from the house and which would have its own driveway. He perused the want ads in the newspaper and found someone who wanted their garage torn down in exchange for the lumber, so he and I did that together one Saturday, hauling home the free lumber in our trailer. I pulled out a lot of nails that day.

Dad asked me to clear the site of small trees and brush so we could lay a foundation. I was almost done with the job when I got a painful surprise. I was attacking the last bit of brush with a sickle. Just before my sickle hit the brush, I saw that it was heading directly for a wasp's nest. Way too late to stop the swing, I made tracks for our back door. It was 200 feet away, but the adrenaline kicked in and I ran like mad, yelling out of fear and being chased by a swarm of angry wasps. I got stung a bunch on my neck, but Mom fixed me up and pretty soon I was back out there to finish the job.

We had to get a water line over to the cabin from our house, so I volunteered to dig the ditch. Dad wanted it dug 18 inches deep and it must have been close to a hundred feet long. About 20 feet from the house I ran into a tree root which was really hard to chop through with the shovel. I finally gave the shovel one last try with all my might before I was going to go for the axe. As the shovel hit I saw sparks fly and heard a huge crackling sound. As it turns out, it was no tree root. It was the 220-volt underground cable coming from the street. My shovel had shorted it out. The current had burned a u-shaped gap in the shovel blade and I could smell ozone. Dad was glad I'd found the 220-volt line; he had always wondered where it was buried. I was just glad I wasn't history.

At school, being in the high school band kept me busy and provided all kinds of fun and challenging experiences. When I was a sophomore we did an exchange trip with the West Valley High band in Spokane—fourteen hours round trip on a bus, a joint concert with their band and an overnight in the home of one of their band's baritone players. And two weeks later, they visited us to do the same thing. I played in solo contests each of my three years at Clover Park. Mr. Taylor would choose the music, always a challenging piece. I'd practice it for weeks, memorize it, and then perform it with piano accompaniment. I was nervous playing in front of the judges, and my knees would start shaking in the middle of the performance. I think it bothered Mom more than it bothered me. Despite the knee trembling, I managed to receive the highest score each year.

I was also picked to play in the all-state band in my junior and senior years, and that was an adventure. You'd travel to another high school somewhere in the state early on a Saturday morning, meet other band kids, practice a good part of the day with them, and put on a concert that evening. I also played solos on my horn in church two or three times a year, for YFC meetings downtown on Saturday nights, and once for Tacoma's city-wide Easter sunrise service at Wapato Park.

Band also provided the backdrop for my third fight with the same guy in four years. Bill, who had a bit of a temper, sat next to me in band. He and I were good friends, and I had a tendency to tease him. Bill could go from being happy to being very angry, just like that and he'd start swinging. It didn't matter if we were in class or not. All three fights he started with me were in a classroom—one in the seventh grade, one in the ninth, and this one in my junior year. I don't remember what I said, but he charged me with fists flying. I stuck my knee up, and it was all over. I was much more of a lover than a fighter. For the next three weeks when I'd greet him in the morning (band was first period) he'd smile broadly, while under his breath and very quietly call me all kinds of quite profane names. I'd just smile back and say "thank you." Other than these small interludes, we were good buddies. We even dated the same girl in our senior year, at different times of course. He loved Ogden Nash and memorized some of his quotes. His favorite was, "A woman is only a woman, but a good cigar is a smoke." Unfortunately, Bill died in Vietnam just six years after we graduated.

The other guy in our baritone section was Tom. Tom was one of those guys who was probably a genius, but didn't do well in school. He learned by *doing*. While he was a bit eccentric, he was fun and loyal. After high school, he started college at MIT, then transferred to the University of Washington. But somehow he couldn't make himself go to class, so he ended up quitting. He's still one of the brightest guys I know. Tom's dad drove a new 1958 blue Dodge station wagon which Tom got to drive sometimes. I use the term "drive" loosely. When Tom was at the wheel, you just hung on. He'd found a road somewhere near Lake Louise where new houses were being built. The road wasn't paved yet, and resembled a roller coaster. Tom would crest the biggest hill going sixty-five and all four wheels would get air. I only did this with him twice—it was way too risky. Tom also installed an air horn on the car. On Saturday nights he'd cruise Pacific Avenue in downtown Tacoma, looking for a drunk to enter the crosswalk at a stoplight. He'd wait until the poor guy was directly in front of the car and give him a blast on the horn. We would laugh for the next mile at the antics of the surprised and very wide-awake drunk. Not very nice.

I never was short on friends in high school. There were the great bunch of guys I ate lunch with in the cafeteria— guys I walked the halls with after. There were guys from church who were good buddies. There were guys in the band. But in addition, both my sisters were my friends in high school — Judy during my sophomore and junior years until she went off to college in Portland for my senior year — and Pat during my senior year after she had returned home from her three years in Chicago. Both of them were always caring toward me. Both had been on the student council at school and both held the position of student body treasurer in their senior year.

Summers continued to be filled with mowing lawns in the morning and spending sunny afternoons swimming at American Lake with friends when I could. The beach was about a mile and a half away. I'd always walk. The lake was so relaxing and the atmosphere felt intoxicating. Once I was there by myself when I saw some older guys harassing some little kids. I approached the guys and asked them to leave the kids alone, causing one of them to challenge me to a fight. I said I didn't want to fight—I just wanted him to quit picking on the little kids, but apparently that wasn't going to work. Meanwhile, his buddy snuck up behind me and grabbed both of my arms, allowing the first guy to punch me in the face. Immediately I lost my glasses which landed in the water. I told them unless they retrieved my glasses I'd come after them when it wasn't two against one. They dove in and found them. Years later, at the University of Washington, I was having a snack down on University Ave and the guy next to me at the counter turned out to be the one who'd hit me in the face. He looked at me, smiled, and said, "I remember you. I beat you up once at American Lake." I told him his memory was hazy and that he'd only gotten the one punch in because his buddy had held my arms behind my back. We parted amicably.

The summer between my junior and senior year, I was urged by my girlfriend at the time, Nancy, into attending summer camp with her at the Firs, a Christian camp on Lake Whatcom in Bellingham. She and I had recently begun our relationship again and she didn't want to go to camp alone. Even though we had an amiable split soon after arriving at the camp, I ended up loving that week at the Firs. I learned how to waterski and hung out most of the time with a friendly guy from our cabin who was also serious about his faith. And within several days, I picked up a different camp girlfriend for the week, Greta. Greta was an attractive Norwegian exchange student who'd arrived in the U.S. only a week prior to camp. After camp, we exchanged letters our whole senior year.

When I got home from camp, I told Dad that I'd learned to waterski and shared how much fun I'd had learning the sport. I think I told him it was pretty difficult (which it really isn't) and asked him if he'd like to try it some time. My friend Ken lived on American Lake and took me waterskiing a few times after school started in September, so I arranged for Dad to give it a try after work one night.

I don't know what I was expecting—but he was a natural. He did a dock start, getting up on his first try, and managed to avoid getting wet! He skied a few big loops on the lake and then Ken drove him back, closer to the dock. Dad let go of the rope at exactly the right time, coasted to the dock, grabbed it, and turned around and sat on it. Again, all without getting wet. He turned to me, grinned, and said, "That wasn't so hard." He was 48 and still very coordinated. I was impressed.

That next spring, Gary Thomas invited me to waterski behind his boat on Steilacoom Lake after school. I was excited—so excited that I forgot to take off my glasses! Gary drove the boat through the opening under the bridge which crosses the lake and I skied under it. After 10 minutes or so, I got a little cocky, took a tumble, and remembered just before I hit the water that I still had my glasses on. They drowned and I drove home half blind.

Dad was the one who taught us all how to drive. He had me drive in our circular driveway a few times before going on public roads. The summer after my sophomore year, about four months before I turned 16, I got my learner's permit and dad kicked off my lessons in our '52 Oldsmobile. Driving the Olds was honestly pretty easy. But he wanted to make sure I knew how to drive a stick shift, so once I was driving decently in the Olds, I started to practice in our '47 Studebaker. That, too, was pleasant except for one time. I had come to a halt at a stop sign on the top of a little hill at the corner of Interlaaken Drive and Washington Blvd. I stopped, but then realized I didn't know how to start again because my left foot was on the clutch pedal and my right foot was holding the brake pedal down. If I took my right foot off to put it on the accelerator pedal, the car would coast backward—and there was a car in back of me. Dad wasn't particularly helpful when I asked him what to do. He never called me *Son*, but he did that day and I didn't like it. He said simply, "Drive, Son. Drive." So I did, and somehow managed to do the necessary footwork. It wasn't as hard as it seemed.

When my 16th birthday rolled around, I took my driver's test and flunked it. I didn't notice that I was driving on a street that bordered the back of a school, and didn't slow down enough. Thus, I experienced an unhappy entrance into the adult world of driving. I retook it a week later on the following Saturday—and this time I passed.

I still had some things to learn, however—and I learned one of them the following Friday when I took the car out alone for the first time at night. I was at a gathering with some friends and someone mentioned that the girl I was interested in wasn't there. I realized he was right, and offered to go get her. My friend, Paul, said that he wanted to get her. So we both rushed for the door, got in our cars and sped off. I was determined to get there before he did and pretty soon I was stupidly speeding down the road. Long story short, I didn't know the road. It made an abrupt ninety degree turn, and I didn't. I put the car in a big slide, hit a ditch, and abruptly stopped. All four wheels were bent a little from the slide, and the back passenger window on my side was broken. Paul stopped to cheer me up, but it didn't work. I drove the car to a station on Gravelly Lake Drive where a friend put it up on the hydraulic lift to see if there was any damage underneath. There wasn't.

The real damage, however, was that I lied to Dad about what had happened—I concocted a story about a drunk coming around a corner and forcing me into the ditch. It was so wrong, but I lived with the lie, and Dad chose to believe me. Decades later, someone brought it up at a family reunion and, with a twinkle in his eye, Dad asked me what really happened that night. I could feel my face turn red all over again. I learned a lot from this incident of double stupidity. Never take chances with a vehicle. And never lie. I should have had the integrity to be accountable for my own action.

But God was working on me. At the church we attended, there was a tall, fun, 28-year-old Minnesotan named Ed Warner who was a telephone lineman. I think he kind of liked my sister, Pat. He asked my friend Rick and me if we would like to meet with him once a week and encourage each other in our Christian faith. I was a senior and Rick, a sophomore. He suggested that we grab a hamburger together, talk about life, and memorize some scripture together. Rick and I both liked the idea, and we liked Ed. He was a great influence in my young life and Rick and I both looked forward to our weekly times. One weekend the three of us camped out on the Oregon coast.

I also went to a men's Bible study on Monday nights for a few months my senior year. We'd meet in Don Woods' kitchen—four of us—and study the book of I John together. Both this time spent with Don and the times shared with Ed let me be side by side with men who were serious about following Jesus. I caught their contagious excitement about the scriptures and knowing Christ, so I purchased a packet of verses from the Navigator organization, and worked on memorizing them. I was beginning to learn the truth that the Christian life was not about performance. It was about a relationship.

The youth group at our church didn't have an adult sponsor my senior year, and so I was asked to take over the reins of the group. We met at the church at six pm. on Sunday nights, and I was responsible for the content and running all the meetings. For me, it seemed a bit much, but I was able to pull it off. I was relieved when the year ended.

I liked three different girls in high school—no long-term relationships, usually they lasted just a month or two at a time. The fall of my senior year I began dating Bobby Jean. With that name you'd think she was either a country singer or that she grew up in Mississippi, but neither was the case. She was in my homeroom class and was vivacious and spirited. Our first few dates were to our high school football games. She was on the drill team, and I was a band guy, so we didn't get to sit together during the games. The game was usually over around 10 p.m., and afterwards we'd grab a burger and fries at a drive-in and I'd drive her home to University Place—about 20 minutes from our house.

The first week I didn't get home until quite late, and Mom told me that from then on I should plan to be home no later than one a.m. I agreed, but the next week, I didn't get in until closer to two. I very carefully drove the car past the house, having already turned the engine off, and with the door open, so as to minimize the noise and not awaken Mom. I knew which stairs squeaked, so avoided those and hit the sack thinking I hadn't woken her up. Wrong. The next morning she let me know that she knew exactly when I'd gotten in, and that it was not by the time we'd agreed on. She told me that if it happened again, I'd lose car privileges for the next weekend. The next Friday night my timing wasn't any better, so while I did all the quiet things, she knew full well that I'd come in well after one again. In the morning she told me I wouldn't be driving the car the following weekend.

This is where it gets embarrassing. I put on my most narcissistic, adolescent self and decided that if she was going to ruin my love life by not letting me have the car, I just wouldn't talk to her. So all of Saturday went by and I didn't say anything to her—I was going to show her. Sunday came and went, and things began to become awkward. Monday morning, she handed me my lunch as I headed off to school and I didn't say "thank you" or even look at her. I realized that I'd started something mean and foolish, but didn't have the courage to apologize and end it. Fortunately, Dad came to the rescue. He caught me in the hallway as he got home from work, gave me the most serious look he'd ever given me, got very close to my face, and told me in no uncertain terms to go in the kitchen right then and apologize to Mom. I did and we both cried and hugged. I was so very wrong to have disrespected my kind and caring Mom like that. But neither Mom or Dad ever brought it up again.

Mom continued to grace our home with cheer, love, kindness and common sense. She wrote all the bills. She carried on active correspondence with many people—her siblings, her best friend from her working years in Chicago before she was married, her own mother, and whichever kid was in college at the moment. She also did all the laundry. Judy helped her with grocery shopping on Saturday mornings and with a lot of the housework. When Dad got home from work at night, he'd often grab a 15-minute nap on the couch before Mom served dinner to all of us. Because she made dinner, one of us kids would set the table, and two kids would wash and dry the dishes each night. Mom kept up her steady habit of reading a Bible verse to us as we left for school in the morning and saying a quick prayer for us.

During the spring of my senior year I applied for admission to two colleges—Wheaton College in Illinois, and the University of Washington (UW) in Seattle. Wheaton cost $2000 a year and UW cost $1000, including tuition, room, board, and books. I was accepted by both, but was concerned about the cost. I knew Dad's take-home pay was under $7000 a year, and he was already supporting Judy in her first year at Multnomah in Portland. He and Mom did have rent money coming in from the apartment over the garage and the rental cabin Dad had built on the property, but I was still worried.

I caught Dad in the dining room on a Saturday morning and posed the question to him about which college I should choose. I told him the costs and reasons for going to either, shared my concerns about money, and asked him what I should do. He said, "Joe, you choose the one you want to attend and we'll make it work. I'll get a part-time job if I need to, and you can work while you're there. Together we can make it." I didn't know the word "palpable" then, but I palpably felt this huge burden lifted from my back. And then I chose UW, because it offered options in engineering while Wheaton didn't. Dad's words, "Together we can make it," gave me such peace. I didn't worry about it again. It was very similar to God saying to us in the scriptures so many times—"Don't be afraid because I will be with you."

At the end of each school year, Mr. Taylor would treat the band to a picnic after school on a Friday afternoon a week before school got out. We always held our picnics at a place called "High Dive" on a lake in Sumner. High Dive's dock had platforms which you could jump off of at heights of 10, 20, 30, 40, and 50 feet. Our band was filled with athletes, and it seemed to be a tradition that the senior guys would jump off the 50-foot platform. When I'd been a sophomore and junior I had watched them and told myself that when I was a senior, I'd jump off, too. (Something about manhood here?) Anyway, I was now the senior and I was determined to jump off the 50 foot one. So I worked up to it, jumping first off the 10-, 20-, 30-, and 40-foot ones. I put a tee-shirt on to soften the water's blow, climbed to the 50-foot platform, and spent about a full minute working up the nerve. Finally, I made the jump, survived, and kept the tradition going.

I walked at graduation on a Friday evening in June, 1959 with a GPA of 3.495— just shy of the 3.5 required to be considered an "honor graduate." Mom had always wanted me to have that honor, but I didn't quite make it. In my senior year I was placed in an English honors class where Mrs. Gibson required extra work for the top grade. I chose to do only the assignments, and that was why my name didn't appear on the commencement program in that special list of "honor grads." I ended up ranked 22nd in a class of 369.

Early the following Monday morning, I sat on our back steps feeling like the rest of my life was staring me in the face. High school was over. I was 17, and in three months I'd be leaving home to be out there in the big world. I hoped I could measure up, but I wasn't sure. Then I remembered a song.

In church the day before, a beautiful song had been sung—the words of which were a takeoff on Jesus' words in Matthew 10. "His eye is on the sparrow and I know he watches me." Those words came to my mind as I was sitting there, and they were a solid comfort. So I prayed, "God, I'm scared, and I don't know what's ahead, but I give you my life. I will really try to seek you and trust you. And thank you that you will be watching out for me."

CHAPTER 4
Dawg Days

IT WAS THE TOUGHEST goodbye I'd ever said. Dad had driven me up to Seattle on Monday morning, September 21, 1959, to drop my belongings off at the University Christian Union (UCU) house on fraternity row, a Christian fraternity house that would be my home for the next four years. My belongings were packed in a trunk and an old suitcase. Dad and I grabbed lunch together at a cafe on University Avenue. Then, after walking to a bank where he helped me open an account, he dropped me off in front of Guggenheim Hall on the UW campus where I would be taking a math placement test. As we shook hands and said goodbye, each of us knew that life for me would never be the same. Even though we were both close to tears, we managed to hold our emotions in check. Thirty Septembers earlier, Dad had said goodbye to his parents and headed off to college as a freshman. Now it was my turn. I even had his old slide rule from his years at the University of Illinois.

That first day was memorable. Along with excitement and anticipation, I was a little nervous and scared. I'd never been a fearful individual, but I had questions. I was just 17. Could I make it on my own? Was I smart enough? How would I do on the math placement test? But I did what I had to do, reported to the right office, took the test and passed it easily. My end of summer study recommended by Mrs. Lackey had paid off. The math professor who administered the test (and who highly resembled an Irish gnome) told me that I had done well and would be able to skip college algebra.

I walked back to the UCU house late that afternoon. I had come to school a week before classes started because I was going to be in the Husky marching band and there was a home football game against Idaho that coming Saturday to prepare for. But coming a week early meant that the house was empty except for an alumnus who was living there for the summer. I bumped into him in the kitchen and asked him where I could possibly get meals this next week. He said I could buy some groceries from the local market and cook for myself, or I could try a boarding house up the street to see if they'd take me for a week. I opted for the boarding house and ended up eating there that week. Meals were decent, but it felt lonely to eat with strangers.

The next morning I walked down to the music building, checked in as a new guy, got an instrument and a uniform, and met Bill Cole, the director. What a good man he turned out to be. He'd played trumpet in the Harry James Band in his younger days, and was now the well-loved director of UW's marching band. He was both cordial and welcoming and let me know that Mr. Taylor, my high school band director, had told him about me and that he was looking forward to having me in the band. That entire first week was spent down on the practice field beside Husky Stadium learning the music and formations for the Idaho game.

The highlight at those practices was meeting Hank Mathews. Like me, he was an incoming freshman majoring in engineering, and he, too, would be living in the UCU house. Hank was outgoing and friendly. His friendship was an example of God's care for us even when we are unaware. He was to be one of my closest friends for the next several years and is one of my pals today sixty years later. After the game on Saturday, I drove with Hank to the Firs in Bellingham, where the rest of the guys in the house had gone for a weekend retreat.

The UCU House had 12 rooms and was home to 24 guys. Established in the 1930's, it was in a great location on the corner of 16th and 47th in the University district. The house was a brick Tudor-style home. I had heard about it in the spring of my senior year at Clover Park, applied ,and got in. The guys were mostly really good guys—all Christians. It ended up being a great place to live. UW was on the quarter system with three quarters a year, and every quarter we would change roommates— the first two quarters of each year, the upperclassmen would room with freshmen.

Two guys came up to me the first night and said a little ominously, "Good luck. I hear you're rooming with Brian." I soon found out why. Brian tended to be on the self-righteous and condescending side. But I settled in and put up with him. I figured it was only for ten weeks plus finals, and I was a peacemaker anyway. Brian was a junior and was engaged to a girl at Seattle Pacific College. Hank was also engaged to a girl there, even though he was only a freshman. Brian often pestered Hank, telling him that he was way too young to be engaged.

One day Hank felt he'd had enough, so he decided to pull a prank on Brian. As house manager, Brian had the responsibility for making sure all the physical details of the house ran smoothly. So Hank and I got our heads together and we began complaining to Brian that the second story bathroom was out of toilet paper too often and that he should do something about it. A day later Hank smeared a melted Hershey bar all over Brian's towel and told him—with a straight face—that he'd run out of toilet paper after going number two and that he was really sorry, but he'd had to use someone's towel instead. Brian didn't think it was funny at all, but the rest of us sure did. Hank married his fiancé over spring break his sophomore year, ironically about the same time that Brian's fiancé broke up with him.

The academic part of school proved to be a challenge that first year. My GPA started out at 2.9 the first quarter, slid to a 2.6 the second, and plunged to 2.0 the third—not an encouraging pattern. As an engineering major, I had a lot of class hours. The second quarter I was in class or in a lab 30 hours every week. Wednesdays that quarter were particularly crazy for me—I spent ten hours in class and lab. But I'm getting ahead of myself.

All incoming engineering students had to take a one-hour class that first quarter called Engineering

Orientation, held in Guggenheim Hall's theater. First off, the professor told the hundreds of us sitting there that an engineering degree was extremely tough and that many of would not make it. He followed that up by asking us to take a look at those around us—and explained that half of us wouldn't be there next year. That wasn't fun to hear. I sure wanted to be one of those who would make it. My very first class was Engineering Problems on the second floor of Miller Hall in the quadrangle. Dr. Boehner, our professor, was an older, serious professor with a German accent. For most of us, the cloudy weather combined with our professor's somber face and the prediction that half of us wouldn't be there next year was all a bit foreboding.

But one of the great things about being in the house was that there were upperclassmen who were engineering majors. Every one of them was willing to help when one of us didn't understand how to tackle a problem. That first quarter in particular, I often sought out their help. A month after school started, I managed to go home for the weekend because there was no home game that weekend to play for. There was a particular section of Calculus which I didn't really understand, and I asked Dad for his help, like I had done occasionally in high school. He studied the book for awhile, shook his head and said that I'd gone beyond what he could help me with. I remember thinking, "Wow, if he can't get it, how in the world am I going to?"

UW in those days had a requirement that you take three quarters of PE your first year. Another requirement was that you had to know how to swim before you graduated. If you didn't know how to swim, your first PE class had to be a beginning swim class. So the first day of our PE class each of us guys had to strip down to his birthday suit and jump in the pool. The object was to prove that we could swim by treading water for five minutes. It must have been a ridiculous sight—dozens and dozens of naked freshman guys treading water all at the same time in very crowded waters, flailing our arms around, trying not to hit each other. And most of us were chuckling a bit nervously the whole time. ("Sorry, I didn't mean to kick you there!")

Another requirement UW had in those days was a commitment to Reserve Officer Training Corps (ROTC) for all able-bodied male students. You could choose Army or Air Force, and you were required to take a one-hour class for two years, plus drill once a week. You could then opt, if you wished, for two additional years and two summer sessions which would lead you to an officer's commission on graduation. (All the Navy ROTC students were selected ahead of time and were granted a full scholarship plus stipend for a four-year commitment.) Most of us, including me, who just wanted the two required years to be easy, joined Air Force ROTC.

Every Thursday morning I'd don my blue uniform and attend class. I never had to go to drill because I was in the marching band, and we were only required to play for the Governor's Day ceremony in the spring. We had inspection occasionally, and our hair was to be cut and our shoes shined. One time that first quarter my hair was a little long, but I was reluctant to spend $1.50 on a haircut. Hank mentioned that he had cut hair before, so I let him cut mine. Looking myself over after he was done, I discovered bald spots all over the side of my head where he had clipped it too close. The inspecting Air Force officer chuckled and shook his head when it came time for my inspection. Hank told me later he hadn't cut anybody's hair before, but just figured that he could and that I'd make a good guinea pig.

Because I'd only had a few jobs that summer, my folks were paying for my entire freshman year. Tuition was $71 per quarter that first year and room and board at the UCU house was $180 per quarter. Books for the year were an additional $100. Mom sent me $5 a month for spending money which went entirely for razor blades and haircuts. I never bought anything extra. Mom always felt badly about only being able to afford to send that small amount. I was just grateful to be there and amazed that they were managing to pay those big bills.

Being a member of the Husky Marching Band was really enjoyable but required a significant investment of time. That first year we played for seven games, including the Rose Bowl. We practiced every Thursday and Friday from three until five in the afternoon, rain or shine. And on Saturday mornings when there was a home game, we'd show up in our uniforms at 8 a.m., practice till 11:30, walk up for a free lunch at the Student Union Building, and then walk back down for our pre-game show after lunch. We'd march on the field before the game to play the national anthem, we'd play during the game, perform the half-time show, and after the game I'd walk the mile back home up the hill to our house. Lots of camaraderie, friendship, exercise, and fun. I've never forgotten the thrill of playing "The Star Spangled Banner" in front of 65,000 people before every game. It always moved me.

The band played for one away game during the regular season which was always a great adventure. We usually took buses, but one year we took the train down to San Francisco and back to play for the University of California, Berkeley game. Several years later our last game of the year was selected to be the NCAA game of the week. Someone in the band came up with the great idea of honoring our director, Bill Cole, with the last half-time formation. Instead of doing what was planned we would all play "Thanks for the Memories," while spelling out "Bill Cole" on the field. Obviously, we had to carry it off without him or his assistant knowing about it, so we had a secret practice on the field the night before the game. I was in a position to see his face as things changed right in front of him in this nationally televised game. His expression went from shock to panic, to throwing up his hands and grinning. The stadium announcer and the TV announcers were in on the gig and we carried it off well. Bill was quite the guy and we were all so pleased to be able to honor and thank him.

Our UCU house fielded intramural teams for flag football, basketball and fast pitch softball. I played on the football team and softball team each year. The football games were played on dirt fields which covered a former garbage dump. The fields were just north of Hec Edmundson Pavilion and Lake Washington was only a hundred yards away. So there were sounds of seagulls and smells of the garbage dump coming through the mud. We always won our league, because they would place us in one of the easier ones, and then typically we would play Navy ROTC in the playoffs and lose to them. They were usually all jocks.

Monday nights at the house we all dressed in ties and coats for dinner as did the other fraternities. After dinner we'd have an interesting Bible study led by George Mathews, Hank's dad, who had lived in the house 20 years earlier. I looked forward to those nights. Following the study, we'd retire to the ping pong room and have a short house business meeting run by our house president. The only tough thing about Monday nights was that you couldn't really do any studying until 8:30 p.m. or so. We also dressed up on Wednesday nights for dinner. Occasionally at that dinner we'd go around the table and give guys a chance to recite any Bible verses they may have memorized recently. When I was a sophomore my buddy, Jim Clifton, who was my favorite-ever roommate, and a guy I would room with after I graduated, got into a bit of trouble at the verse recitation. Not trouble, actually, just a bit of awkwardness. He'd discovered this obscure verse in 2nd Chronicles 26:18. "At Parbar westward, four at the causeway and two at Parbar." We both memorized it to be funny, and he quoted it the next Wednesday night. The house president, Neal, a pretty straight-laced guy, came down on him a bit. Jim and I and everyone else thought it added a little levity to the dinner.

We had house officers—a president, vice president, treasurer, social secretary, and house manager. The house manager split up all the duties in the house so each member, except the president and the house manager, had his particular duty to perform each week. These responsibilities ranged from cooking breakfast, setting the table and serving lunch and dinner (we had a cook, Mrs. Welch, for those two meals), doing the dishes for each meal, vacuuming, cleaning the bathrooms, washing the kitchen and dining room floors, and cooking a lunch meal on Sundays. Our house duties provided a lot of camaraderie and allowed friendships to deepen because you were usually paired up with other guys.

Once when heading home from class before lunch, I realized I was going to be late in setting the table unless I really sped up. So I got to the big intersection at 45th and 17th where hundreds of students would wait for the proper light to cross. Because I was in a hurry, I ignored the light, waited for an opportunity, and sprinted across. Just at that moment, a motorcycle cop sped up the hill. He put his siren on, motioned me to the curb, and gave me a $2 jaywalking ticket. Needless to say, I was late for setting the table.

I got into the habit of getting up early enough to read scripture and pray a bit at my desk each morning before heading off to class. I'd not done that regularly before.

I remember discovering some great truths about God's grace and kindness—especially from the books of John, Romans, and Psalms.

About a month into the fall quarter, I had a rough week. On that Monday I took my first calculus mid-term and was pretty sure I'd flunked it. On Tuesday, I lost my slide rule, which, as I'd mentioned, had been my Dad's and would cost $30 to replace. On Wednesday, I woke up feeling like I'd been kicked in the tailbone. It hurt badly enough that I called Mom to talk with her about it, and she told me it was most likely a cyst on my tailbone which our doctor had identified years earlier. When you get to be 18 -20 years old, they very often become infected and need to be drained, and then removed through surgery. To top this great week off, at breakfast on Thursday Hank offered me this blue pill, which he said worked great for pain. He said both his dad and he had used it. I was a little hesitant, but gave in and took the pill. Late that afternoon after my basketball class, I had to relieve my bladder, so did so in one of those trough kind of urinals. It came out the most dazzling bright blue you've ever seen, flowed downstream in front of another guy, also using the urinal. He looked at me with a "What the heck is that?" kind of look. By that time I had put two and two together and realized that Hank's blue pill had dyed my urine. I muttered something to the guy about taking a blue pill. I'm sure he thought I was in serious trouble.

Anyway, the week ended up going better than I thought it would after such a rough start. We got our calculus tests back and even though I'd gotten a 64, it was a B, because my professor graded on the curve. I checked with Lost and Found in the Student Union building, and was thrilled to learn that someone had turned my slide rule in. And, Hank's pill was a temporary dye. I was glad I hadn't had too many weeks like that one.

The cyst, though, was serious, and made it painful for me to sit in one position for a long period of time. We were slated for a band trip to California to play for the Cal Berkeley game a week later. That proved to be one long, uncomfortable bus ride. We left early on a Friday morning and returned at six on Monday morning, just in time to grab a quick breakfast and head down to class. Two weeks later was Thanksgiving break, and my dear Mom had me lie on my stomach a lot while she put hot compresses on it. A few weeks later it healed up, and I had it operated on and removed over spring break that year. Speaking of Mom, she was a great nurturer. She wrote me twice a week all during college. Getting her letters was always such a joy. And I knew that she prayed for me regularly.

Final exams that first quarter were memorable only because of calculus. Mr. Minty, our instructor, was a bit strange, as were many of my math professors at the U. But at least he was likable. The test was scheduled for eight a.m. on Monday of finals week and was my very first college final. I was prepared, but anxious. Most of us arrived ten minutes early just to be safe. Eight o'clock arrived and we began looking at the clock. No Mr. Minty. At ten after eight the banter started. Still no Mr. Minty.

An upperclassmen mentioned that you didn't have to stay more than 15 minutes if a professor failed to show up for class—even for a final. Most of us were taking no chances, and we stuck around, even though after 20 minutes some left. A couple of the students went to the blackboard at that point and started writing humorous and crazy problems on it. We were all chuckling when Mr. Minty finally rolled in, full of apologies. He gave us some good news. He allowed that he had messed up and that none of us would flunk. He also said that if we were satisfied with the grade we already had, we could leave without taking the final and that grade would be ours. But if we wanted to improve our grade, we could stay and take the final. I knew I had a B already, and was happy with that, so left with a smile on my face and walked back to the house to study for my next final.

Christmas break was fun because the Huskies had won the Pac Eight Conference. We were headed to the Rose Bowl to play the favored Big Ten Wisconsin Badgers. The Huskies hadn't been to a Rose Bowl since 1944. So the day after Christmas, the band boarded a plane—my very first commercial airplane ride—for Los Angeles. Hank and I got to room together for the week in a UCLA dorm. The experience was incredible. We practiced our routines at UCLA for the first few mornings and afternoons, leaving us free to take trips to Knott's Berry Farm and Disneyland on other days. We even put on a parade at Disneyland. Early on January 1st, we got in line for the Rose Parade near the corner of Green Street and

Orange Grove Boulevard in Pasadena. It was a very cold morning. We then marched and played tunes during the five-mile trek to Pasadena High. Bill Cole had stashed a bunch of cases of coke for us there. By the end of the parade, I'd worn holes in my leather-soled ROTC shoes and the next year had wet feet every time I wore my uniform in the rain. After our part was over, we headed to the game nearby. It did not disappoint. The Huskies proved the prognosticators wrong, and beat the Badgers 44-8.

A couple of other classroom stories from that first year. The Engineering Orientation class met at one in the afternoon once a week. This was the class taught by the same professor who had told us that half of us wouldn't be around the following year. Early afternoon classes are typically hard for some people (like me!) to stay awake in because their bodies are busy digesting their lunch. But this guy didn't care about any of that. When a student would start to doze off, the prof would throw a piece of chalk at him. His aim was good, so I always made sure I sat toward the back. To this day, I still get sleepy after lunch if I'm sitting in a meeting or a classroom.

My second quarter calculus class was taught by Dr. Hano, a quality teacher with a pretty heavy Japanese accent. He provided us with some accidental humor on more than one occasion. When it came to explaining the "partition" concept in Calculus, he pronounced it "Pa' ti shun." Most of us figured out that he meant partition, but not everyone got it. After several days of discussing partition theory a student raised his hand and told Dr. Hano that he was very confused. "What is this Pa' ti shun you keep mentioning. I couldn't find it in the book." The rest of us laughed at the poor guy because we'd already figured it out and as Dr. Hano tried to explain, it just got funnier.

Dr. Hano had a routine. He'd enter the fourth floor classroom, lean against one of the tall windows, light a cigarette and then commence with his lecture. One morning he started through his routine without noticing that the window he always leaned on was open. He started to lean backwards toward the open window, caught himself from falling out at the last second (to our relief) and then giggled, very relieved and embarrassed at the same time. To cap it off, he nervously tried lighting the wrong end of his cigarette. By that time, we all were howling. From that day on when he entered class, he'd walk over to the window and make sure it was closed before he lit his cigarette, and he and the class would chuckle together.

The term, "freshman 15," hadn't come into being yet, but that first year I gained 20 pounds and two inches in height. I'd begun the year at 135 pounds and five feet nine, and I ended up at 155 and a hair short of five feet eleven.

Dad lined up a job for me the summer between my freshman and sophomore years. A large contractor was building 856 houses for military families at Fort Lewis and I ended up being the "boy" for the general contractor.

By "boy" I mean that I did whatever they asked me to do and the jobs varied all over the place. The big news for me was that I was making $3 an hour. I had never made more than a buck an hour before. The job meant that I could pay for all of my sophomore year. In fact, Mom even borrowed some money from me at one point. I thought that was really cool. She handled all the family finances.

One wild memory from that job: Late one Friday afternoon I was asked to head to the tide flats of Tacoma with a company pickup to get a load of trim from a mill. I found the mill, loaded the trim all up and headed back to Fort Lewis, pretty anxious to return as quickly as I could because it was Friday night. Right off the bat I hit a red light. When the light turned green, I accelerated a bit quickly and within seconds my load slid off the truck bed and was strewn out all over the busiest intersection in Tacoma at 5 p.m. on a Friday night. Fortunately, within seconds a providential motorcycle cop appeared on the scene and directed traffic around me until I had everything back in the truck and took off again, much more slowly. Live and learn.

My sophomore year kicked off with none of the trepidation of the previous year. It proved to be a good season of life. My grades that year jumped from the 2.0 of my freshman spring quarter to a 3.5 in the fall, to a 3.7 winter quarter, and a perfect 4.0 my spring quarter. I honestly don't know what made the difference. Maybe I was figuring out how to study. Halfway through the year our house manager had to leave the house and I was asked to take his place—a job which I held for the rest of that year and all of my junior year. In practical terms, it meant that I assigned all the house jobs, but didn't have to do any of them myself. As busy as I was with engineering and band, I was okay with that.

My good friend from high school, Art Volz, came as a freshman to UW and to the UCU house my sophomore year. Art and I spent a lot of time together over the next 3 years. Sometimes on Sunday afternoons, I'd head to his room, or he'd head to mine, one of us would be on the bottom bunk, the other on the top and we'd try to study lying down. We both knew full well that within a short time, we'd both be asleep. Makes me sleepy even thinking about it. In the summers he and I often played tennis together on weekends or after work. We were also members of the house quartet. Art was the bass, Jay Oertli and then Dan Greene were the baritones, several different guys sang second tenor, and I was usually first tenor. We often sang at different house events and sometimes at churches. Jim Clifton was our piano player.

The Huskies won the Pac Eight my sophomore year also, and beat the favored Minnesota Golden Gophers 17-7 in the 1961 Rose Bowl. Again we were given the chance to fly down to LA, march at Disneyland, do the parade, and watch the game. This was the famous Rose Bowl where Cal Tech students pulled off a very ingenious stunt. They snuck into UW's stash of cards for the card section and changed their order so when the announcer announced "University of Washington" the cards spelled out "Cal Tech" instead. It turned out to be a national headline story in the press. In the years since then, I've gotten a lot of mileage out of telling folks that I played in two Rose Bowls for the Huskies. When people look at my size and say, "Wow! How cool! What position did you play?" I surprise them by answering, "Baritone, in the band." It's always good for a cheap laugh.

Bill Cole pulled us together after the last practice before the Rose Bowl to announce the winners of the two awards the band gave out at the end of each season. Much to my surprise, he called my name as one of the winners. I'd won the "Outstanding Returning Bandsman" award which included a year's tuition—$300. That was both a delight and a huge financial help.

That winter quarter I experienced the high point of my academic career at UW. I was taking the second of three physics classes which were required of all engineering students. There were 200 of us studying electrical and magnetic physics in the class. I had some free time late in the afternoon the day before the second mid-term. I felt like I was already well prepared for it, so began reading *Exodus*, by Leon Uris, thinking that I could do a final review for the test that evening. I never ended up doing that review because I just couldn't put the book down. It was one of the best books I'd ever read. I finished the last page late that night and went right to sleep. The next morning the test just flew by and when the grades were posted a couple of days later, I'd scored 183 out of 200, the highest grade in the class.

In the last quarter of my sophomore year, Dad and Mom offered to let me have the '52 Oldsmobile up at school because they had just purchased a newer car. Looking back, it might have been better if they hadn't. Dad had one request. He told me that some of the guys might want to borrow the car and if I trusted them, it would be okay. But I was not to loan the car to Tom Watson under any circumstances. Tom was my high school friend who had been the wild driver. After Tom left MIT, he'd enrolled at UW and was living in our house. I agreed to Dad's stipulation.

But one Saturday night, Tom begged me four times in three hours to borrow the car. He kept coming to my room and asking—saying he absolutely had to straighten something out with his girlfriend. I finally relented, ignoring Dad's explicit order. Dad proved to be right, because, sure enough, Tom put the car in a ditch that night. He assured me that he'd do the repairs on it, but I did have to tell Dad. That wasn't a fun phone call to make. Still can't believe I did that.

On another night, following our house's social event of the year, I was driving my date home to Puyallup from Seattle in the wee hours of the morning. We hadn't been out partying—the event we'd gone to simply hadn't gotten out until very late. I was driving south on old Highway 99 and I was almost the only one on the road. I just wanted to get my date home, drive to my folks' house, and get some sleep. So I was foolishly going 75 in a 50 zone. I saw the flashing red light about a half mile back getting closer. When the officer pulled me over, he didn't look any older than me, but he appeared to be very angry. He issued me a reckless driving ticket because anything over 20 mph over the speed limit can be classified that way. The jurisdiction was under the control of a local justice of the peace—a Judge Thigden. I called and tried to find out the fine several times but was unsuccessful. Later that summer the judge conducted a hearing of which I was given no notification. There was no fine, but I had to buy "high risk" insurance for the next year if I was to drive. I chose not to drive for that next year, because the price for the insurance was prohibitive. Four years later, when I was in grad school at Stanford, Dad mailed me a newspaper article saying that justice of the peace Thigden had been convicted of wrongdoing and had been jailed. Sorry, but it did make me smile.

Spring quarter of my sophomore year I roomed with Jim Clifton. We had the biggest and best room in the house. Jim was the piano player who'd also quoted the odd verse at the dinner table. We quickly developed a fast and enduring friendship. We even painted the room lavender because it was the favorite color of the girl he liked at the moment. I'd done something to Jim which I can't remember, and he gotten me back by taping a fish he'd purchased at Safeway to the back of our room's radiator. The room began to stink with this rotten smell, and it took me a couple of days to discover what it was. I never really understood Jim's reasoning for the prank, because he had to put up with the odor as much as I did!

We just always had so much fun together. Jim was the smartest guy in the house and it must have rubbed off on me because that was the quarter I got my one and only 4.0.

That summer I wasn't able to line up a job, but Dad managed to get me a temporary one which lasted three weeks working for his plumbing crew at Fort Lewis. Dad was in charge of the water supply, sewage system, and garbage disposal at the Fort. I was teamed up with two other temporary guys to clean out the drainage traps all over the north side of the base. We used shovels shaped like soup ladles with long handles. We worked steadily all day long, and the regular plumbing crew guys kept remarking how we were the hardest working guys they'd ever seen. It was a very hot summer with lots of sunshine every day. In the back of one mess hall, we recovered over a hundred pieces of silverware from the drainage trap. The other temporary workers were young guys like me and we made it fun. We got really good at flipping off manhole covers, except for one day when I flipped one off and it came back and landed on my big toe. Painful! Immediately my toenail turned black and pretty soon came off. I went back to work the next day with a hole cut out of the leather in my work shoe because the swollen toe wouldn't fit in the shoe.

After two weeks of that duty, I was assigned to work with a different temporary worker painting a huge culvert pipe which went over a small ravine. The man was older and just plain crude. He used bad language, with profanities every third sentence. I told Dad about the guy that night, and the next day he was history. I hadn't meant to get him terminated, but guessed that Dad was still watching out for me.

My sister, Judy, was home from school that summer and working as a counselor at a camp called Firwood in Bellingham. When my temporary job at the Fort was over, she called and asked if there was any way I could work the rest of the summer with her at the camp because they were a male counselor short. Even though there was to be no pay, I said that I'd love to.

So I spent the rest of the summer of 1961 at Firwood on Lake Whatcom near Bellingham. Firwood was isolated. You either had to walk in about a mile on a path, or boat in. The camp was rustic—little lean-to tent cabins on the side of a hill facing the water, an open-air covered dining hall, an outside small amphitheater with logs for seats, and an island opposite the shore. Each counselor was given a nickname for the summer. Mine was "Winky." Besides having a different group of campers to care for each week, each counselor also taught classes—mine were waterskiing and canoeing. I had ten minutes of training on the canoe before I began teaching, but I caught on quickly and even learned how to waterski on one ski that summer.

I had been asked to bring my horn along with me, and during the second week I learned a lesson in grace. That week our campers were fifth and sixth graders. As we drifted off to sleep the first night, someone had asked a camper in another cabin who had brought a trumpet with him to play taps as the lights were turned off. Unfortunately, he massacred the tune. We were all cringing. So the guys in my cabin urged me to play it also. I did and quite well, I might add. And then the trumpet-playing camper played "Oh When the Saints." So I played it—only better. I was on the third song, when the camp director climbed up the steps to our lean-to. He asked me politely but firmly what I thought I was doing. I told him I was really sorry, and hit the sack. A couple of my older campers, two-year veterans of Firwood, were afraid I was going to be relieved of my duties in the morning.

I didn't sleep very well that night, and the next morning I bumped into the camp director in the shower room. I apologized profusely for my indiscretion and his reply back to me was so gracious. "Hey, don't worry about it, Winky. We learn from our mistakes." And it was over with. Talk about a lesson in forgiveness and grace. I've never forgotten his words and their impact on me.

Each week we took our campers on an overnight. We either hiked out of camp somewhere to a beach a mile or two away, or we took canoes over to the other side of the lake to find an isolated beach. We cooked "wilderness hash" over a fire (the cook had given us a tasty recipe complete with ingredients), slept overnight under the stars, enjoyed a cold breakfast, and returned in the late morning the following day.

On our first overnight everything had gone smoothly. The wilderness hash had been a big hit with the junior high kids and they'd gone to sleep without a hitch. But in the early dawn hours, I became aware of a loud breathing noise and some snorting. It sounded like it was right next to me. There was also a strong pungent smell in the air. I immediately thought, *BEAR!*. I turned my head as slowly and quietly as I could, so I could see what it was, praying that I could somehow get this bear, if that's what it was, out of our camp. Turns out it was a happy milk cow grazing on some grass about three feet from my head. Whew!

A few weeks later, I took my campers—a few high school guys—in the canoes over to the far side of the lake. They were fun kids and we enjoyed a great evening together. A noisy wind and rain storm woke all of us up around three in the morning. Most of the guys were wet already, so I suggested that we go skinny dipping. Why not? They thought it was a great idea. We swam for a bit in the rain and I built a fire to heat up some cocoa. By that time we'd rested our three canoes over a downed tree on one side and a big rock on the other to form a shelter. We were sitting snugly underneath our shelter drinking cocoa and talking, when all of a sudden we heard a deafening, loud, cracking noise and felt the ground shaking. The canoes above us bounced all over the place. We didn't have any idea what was happening.

It turns out that a several-hundred-year-old Douglas fir about ten feet away had decided that he'd lived long enough and had fallen on top of us and our canoes due to the wind and rain. Fortunately, the canoes had afforded us protection and none of us were hurt. Two of the canoes were destroyed, but the third had only a small hole in it. In the morning, I sent two of the campers paddling back to Firwood with a shirt stuffed in the hole to ask the camp to send a boat to come and get us. By the time we returned, we had become quite the heroes around camp. Much to be said for life in the woods.

My junior year was a busy one, in addition to all of the classwork. That fall I was the assistant band manager (which paid $100) and I was in my second year of being the UCU house manager. I also got $12 a game for playing my horn for all the home basketball games. Bill Cole had selected about 25 of us for that responsibility. The previous years the basketball band had been totally volunteer, and this move to pay us guaranteed that enough of us would show up so we sounded reasonable.

Mom enjoyed watching those home games on TV, because the band sat behind one of the baskets and she would watch for me. Mom also became a football fan and began watching all the home games on TV.

In the spring I got a temporary job painting the exterior of an old warehouse on Westlake Avenue overlooking Lake Union. I'd catch a series of buses to get there, and return smelling like paint. I always felt sorry for people sitting next to me on the bus on those rides back. I remember that the paint was blue, and that I worked on memorizing Romans, chapter eight, while I painted.

My first concrete, without-a-doubt, answer to a specific prayer occurred during that year. Looking back from the vantage point of many years, I know for certain that God had answered earlier prayers, but up to that point, my prayers had been of a more general nature. "God—here is my life. Please take it and use it." Or, "Lord, help me to make it here in college." But this time it was different.

One evening I was sitting alone in my room taking stock of my life. For a non-introspective guy, this was pretty rare. What became crystal clear to me that night within just a few moments was that, although my relationship with Christ meant everything to me, I had never really shared my faith with anyone in a straightforward fashion. I'd never laid out, *"Here's what I believe and why. Here's the difference Jesus has made in my life."* My roommate was gone for the evening, so I began to pray seriously that sometime very soon I'd get an opportunity to do exactly that—to just sit down with a friend and tell him about Jesus. I actually got down on my knees and prayed.

After a few minutes, I felt so strongly about it that I went next door to Jay Oertli's room and asked him to pray with me about it. Jay, a great guy from Montana, did just that. And he didn't think I was crazy, which I appreciated. Then I promptly resumed my student mode and went back to studying like normal.

The next morning I woke up, ate breakfast, and headed down to class, having totally forgotten my prayer of the night before. After my 11-o'clock class, I was heading back to the house for lunch, and crossing the quad, I heard somebody yell out my name from about thirty feet away: "Hey Joe!" Turning around, I saw that it was a guy I knew named Bruce.

Bruce had been the UW class president our freshman year who had gained a bit of notoriety during the election. He was a fun guy, outgoing, a little cocky in a good way, and he happened to be Jewish. During the election campaign, Bruce had been perched up in the back seat of a convertible in a parade of candidates running for office, and someone called him a derogatory name.

Bruce responded by flipping the guy off. The story was reported to campus officials and even though he won the election, the "obscene gesture" caused officials to question his right to hold the office. After a week or so, they finally ruled that he was within his rights, and he took office. So Bruce was famous, or infamous, depending on your perspective, and he was a friend of mine. We'd sat next to each other in a few classes and he knew I was a Christian. So I yelled back, "Hi Bruce!"

His next words floored me. He yelled back, still from 30 feet away and with onlookers listening, "Joe, when are you going to tell me about your religion, anyway?" You could have knocked me over with a feather at that point because instantly I remembered my prayer of the night before. My thoughts were, "Wow, God! You really do exist! And you really answer prayer!" (A faithless response as I look back on it.)

So Bruce and I arranged a time to meet in the next several days. I showed up at his apartment, and he sat and listened to me as I presented my sensible and heartfelt version of the Gospel to him. When I was done, he thanked me and said that that was the most logical thing he had ever heard about Jesus. Did he respond? No. But that one incident burned into me that God hears our heartfelt prayers.

I think God had Bruce call out to me in such a clear way just to get my attention. To let me know how real He is and to increase my faith. The last part of Psalm 37:23 says that "He cares about every detail of their lives." (NLT) I was beginning to get that.

Over spring break of that junior year, I had surgery again, just like my freshman spring break. Not for a cyst this time, but for something called a *hydrocele*. It was a male thing, easily fixable and not serious. I had a lot of nice nurses during the several days in the hospital check in on me. They had all been older. A couple of hours before I was scheduled to check out and head home, a lovely, attractive, young nurse walked in wearing her cute white uniform and asked me how I was doing. We had a friendly conversation for five minutes, and I was seriously considering asking her for her phone number so I could take her out. She was really nice.

But before I could ask her, she said, "Guess what I get to do?" I said I had no idea, and then, smiling, she dropped the bomb: "You'll need to turn over because I need to give you an enema before you check out." I was horrified. "Oh, please. Not you. Please. Send in one of the older ones!" I wanted it to be anyone but her. She answered that she was sorry, but it was her job. I obediently turned over, and underwent the procedure. Needless to say, I didn't ask her for her phone number.

During my college years, going to church was a regular part of my week. When I arrived as a freshman, a number of the guys in the house attended a church up on Capitol Hill, so that's where I went too. A few of them had cars which made transportation easy. In my junior year I was asked to teach the church's Sunday school class for seventh and eighth grade boys, and I said yes. Teaching those kids just for a short time on Sunday mornings without getting to know them at home or at school was difficult. So I began to spend time with a few of them during the week to gain their friendship, enter their world, and, honestly, help me be able to survive on Sunday mornings. I didn't put it together at the time, but I was to see later that I was simply being incarnational—just like John described Jesus' entry into our world in the first chapter of his gospel. "So the Word (God) became human and made his home among us." It was God's way of making himself known to us. That principle of entering someone else's world to get to know them and become their friend would stick with me the rest of my life.

Intramural softball that spring quarter was a kick in the pants for me. A big guy named Waite had moved into the house that year, and he was an exceptional softball pitcher. He went on to become the MVP in an industrial league for many years. I was privileged to be in his wedding a year later. The team asked me to be his catcher.

What an experience that was. His pitches had incredible speed and the ball would do all these crazy things just a few feet before hitting the plate. It was delightfully fun and challenging to catch for him, and some of the fingers on my catching hand were pretty sore sometimes. We did very well in the intramural league that spring.

That summer, Dad once again pointed me to a job working for the project manager of a general contractor at Fort Lewis. He had written a letter for me to send to them that spring which was exceptional. I wish I had kept a copy. It had the perfect amount of braggadocio and humility in it. Dad was a good writer, and I got the job. Like the job I'd had two summers previously, my duties varied all over the place. Mom packed me great lunches with a couple of quart jars of ice water to drink, as it was a very hot summer. The construction boss was a blustery little Texan named Napoleon B. Morris. Yes, the B stood for Bonaparte. We all called him Bowie. Bowie was a character. He liked me, maybe because I worked hard and managed to figure out how to do anything he asked. I came in on a weekend once and unloaded a truckload of lumber with our forklift. The company was building 500 houses for soldiers and their families.

I also worked for Bowie over Christmas break during my senior year, too, and got a little sideways with him for a day. His wife, Goldie, had decorated a Christmas tree which we had in our construction shack office. Bowie and Goldie were planning to host a Christmas party at the officer's club on the post for us. He asked another guy and me to take a company pickup truck to haul the tree to the officer's club on a cold, rainy Friday night. My job was to sit in the back and make sure the tree didn't fall over. But after going just about a hundred yards, I was already freezing. So I knocked on the window and told the driver to stop. I secured the tree pretty well, got in the pickup cab, and we took off. The tree promptly fell over. I hopped out to prop it up again, and looked back to see if anybody had seen us. Sure enough, there was Bowie standing on the front porch of the construction shack, jumping up and down waving his arms and using all kinds of colorful language. I got back in the pickup bed and we delivered the tree (which was still in fine shape, by the way) and returned to the office where I got a well-deserved chewing out. He read me the riot act, Texas-style.

The party was that night, and, after what I'd just experienced with Bowie, I didn't feel like going, so stayed home. On Monday morning at work Bowie grabbed me first thing and told me how disappointed he was that I hadn't come—that, yes, I had deserved the chewing out, but that it was just one small incident and that it was over. Then he gave me a bottle of expensive whiskey as a Christmas present. I didn't drink, so gave the bottle to the guy who I'd gotten in trouble with. And Bowie wrote me a bonus check of $250 when I went back to school. He was a good guy. And I learned from my mistake. Obey orders.

I had dated girls sporadically during my first three years of college, but none seriously, at least not until I met

Norma in the spring of my junior year. Norma worked for Shell Oil as a secretary and lived in a spectacular apartment in downtown Seattle on James Street. Her apartment had a sweeping view of Elliot Bay and had a glassed-in swimming pool on the first floor. I was head over heels in love—or like, or something. Norma was fun and beautiful. She was very serious about her faith, and she liked me. We saw each other regularly that spring and the summer that I was working for Bowie Morris. I think I had her on a bit of a pedestal, though, which never works well for very long in any relationship. To make a long story short, she cooled the relationship a bit at the very end of the summer, but we kept dating a bit and I kept holding out hope. On my 21st birthday that November she threw me a fun surprise party at the best Japanese restaurant in Seattle. After that, we dated until Christmas, but then it was pretty much done with. I was sad for a bit, but moved on.

If I thought my junior year had been busy, it honestly didn't hold a candle to my senior year. I had been selected to serve as president of our house that year, with all the accompanying responsibilities. The Husky Marching Band continued to be a significant part of my life and I was voted in as president of the band also. It wasn't an office I ran for, but was voted in anyway. Bill Cole had sent me another letter at the end of the previous season, letting me know I was the recipient of the Senior Bandsman Award. Like the award I'd received a year earlier, this one carried with it a grant of $300 for free tuition for the next year. And I was now the band manager, which paid $300 as well. I continued to play in the basketball band for $12 a game, and for the second year in a row, played my horn in the University brass choir—a select group of brass players at the U. We played all original music written by a well-known composer of brass music who was in residence as an instructor at UW at the time. The income certainly made a difference in helping pay for school.

That fall, the church I was attending also asked me to be president of the college group. I really didn't want to, and turned them down initially, but they continued to press me on it, and I accepted reluctantly. It turned out to be a good year, but Sundays were now full of responsibility instead of being a relaxing weekend day off.

I had bought my first car in July of that year (now that my year of not driving was up) and I so was the owner of a 1953 two-tone Ford Victoria. One of the perks of being president of the house was that I got one of the coveted parking places in our house's 4-car parking lot, which was very convenient. Starting winter quarter of my senior year, I also began working as a draftsman for Boeing and worked 16 hours a week through the end of the school year. I figured out once that because of summer jobs, awards and part-time jobs during my college years, I ended up paying about two-thirds of my total college costs, which I know Dad and Mom were happy about. But I was sure grateful for the part they paid.

When I was home over spring break that year, Dave Stewart, the new pastor of our family's home church in Lakewood asked me out for lunch. I was a bit surprised, because we'd only met a couple of hours before. I was even more surprised when, over lunch, he asked me if I'd be open to coming back in a month and giving the sermon in church at both services. It was a big church and my first thought was, "Why would you ask me?" When I verbalized my question, he said that he knew my folks and the quality of their lives, and had heard that I was committed to following Jesus, and he just thought it would be a good idea. I thanked him for taking a chance on me, and four weeks later, a little nervous, I took my turn in the pulpit. I remember walking around the quiet, dark UW campus late the night before, practicing the sermon. Putting it together, I'd used scripture, borrowed a little bit from here and there, added some of my own thoughts, made sure it was twenty-five minutes long, and then it was done. Dave was obviously a guy who had vision for what the next generation could do.

Living in the UCU house opened up all kinds of avenues for friendship. One of the results for me was that I would be in eight of my housemate's weddings. We'd shared a lot of adventures together. We'd thrown newly engaged guys in frosh pond down in front of Bagley Hall. We'd battled fiercely in water balloon fights with the frat house across the alley, the Betas. We'd engaged in numerous athletic contests and crazy pranks. Once, Jim Clifton and I both wanted to take out the same girl. We decided to wrestle for the privilege. We wrestled until we were so tired we decided to quit and just toss a coin. He won. And the date wasn't even that fun. There had been lots of great memories made in the past four years, and they were fast drawing to a close.

I remember one particularly humorous incident that took place winter quarter of my final year. My roommate at the time, a freshman named Lowell, came in one Sunday night talking a little brashly about how he'd just dropped his girlfriend. A couple of us "more sophisticated" upperclassmen haughtily thought we would teach him a lesson in humility and how to treat women. So we grabbed him, tied him up in a clothes basket, put a baby bonnet on his head, and made a sign to go along with it that said, "I'm all tied up in knots over you." Then we put him in the trunk of my car, drove him to her house in north Seattle, dropped him on her front porch, rang the doorbell, and took off. As we drove away, we watched him wiggle his way off the porch—he was upside down in the tulips next to it when the girl's father answered the door.

The next Thursday night, it was payback time for me. Jim Clifton had warned me that something was up. He didn't know exactly what it was, but said I'd better make myself scarce. The guys were planning a retaliation. So I headed off to the UW library until it closed. By the time I arrived back at the house, it was late. The house seemed eerily quiet. Thinking maybe I was safe, I grabbed a pillow and headed down to the living room where I went to sleep behind one of the couches. All of a sudden I woke up and heard all the guys in the house, whispering: "Hey, we've looked everywhere—the boiler room included—he's just not here. Maybe we'll have to do it tomorrow night." My heart started to pound so hard that I could actually hear it. We'd always talked about taking somebody down to skid row on First Ave in Seattle dressed in a dress, and handcuffing them to a fire hydrant. I was worried they'd do that to me. So I lay there, trying to not breathe loudly, until they finally headed to bed, resigned to doing it the next night instead.

But as they all traipsed upstairs, something came over me. For some reason I'll never understand, I waited until I heard the last footfall die down, then yelled as loud as I could, "SUCKERS!" Boy, did they return in mass immediately. Rob, a big huge lineman for the Husky freshman football team, leaned over the couch, found me, and dragged me out gleefully. "Here he is, guys!" They put me in my own car, drove it down to the ferry dock on Seattle's waterfront, and put me on the last ferry to Bremerton—handcuffed to the steering wheel. Shoot, I didn't even have my wallet or my glasses.

Halfway to Bremerton, one of the ferryboat guys came and let me out, laughing the whole time. The guys had given him the key to the handcuffs. I managed to borrow a dime from a stranger on the boat by explaining awkwardly what had happened. I drove the car off the ferry in Bremerton, found a phone booth, and called the only person I knew in Bremerton. Her name was Wray and she'd been a counselor with me at the Firs in Bellingham 2 years earlier. She gave me directions to her place, and I actually had to get out of the car at every intersection so I could see the street signs, my eyes were that bad.

It was two a.m. by the time I arrived at Wray's house, but even though it was late she was very welcoming and made me coffee. We ended up talking until five. Wray loaned me $3 for the toll on the Narrows Bridge so I could drive the long way around to Seattle. I got back just in time to shower and have breakfast at the house with the guys before I had to head to class at eight. We all had a good laugh about what had happened. That night I had a date with a girl and fell asleep five minutes into the concert. But the lesson was learned—what goes around comes around. Two years ago, we had a 50-year reunion of the UCU guys from our college years—and they were still talking about the time they shipped me out on the last ferryboat to Bremerton handcuffed to the steering wheel of my own car.

I made a mistake my very last quarter at UW and took a three-unit high-powered math class which was beyond differential equations. I had taken "diff e q" as we referred to it, and barely made it out alive. To this day I don't know why I signed up for this more difficult class—I should have taken something easy! To make matters worse, it met at seven in the morning. For the first eight weeks, I made it to every class, but then I slowed the pace a little, making two of the three classes the next week. The final week, I made one class. I knew I was flirting with disaster, but I passed it, gratefully, with a C.

Several weeks before my last finals, the director of Campus Crusade for UW, Gordon Klenck, asked me to meet him for coffee down on University Avenue. He had been a good influence and role model for me the past two years. Gordon made a pitch for me to join the staff of Campus Crusade after graduation. I listened, and while I felt honored, I said no because I felt like I needed to give my engineering education a try. A week later the head of Navigators in Seattle, Elven Smith, asked me if I would consider joining their staff. Jim Clifton and I had really profited spiritually from Elven and the Navigators. Many times we'd enjoyed meals with Elven and his wife, Joyce, in their home. Again, I felt honored, but declined. A week later I accepted an offer from the Boeing Company to be an engineer in Seattle with them, starting July first.

I decided not to go through the graduation ceremony, because I would have had to stick around the campus four more days after my last final. The ceremony itself didn't have much of a draw for me. But walking back up through campus after my last final, I paused and pondered over the fact that my undergraduate days were over. The years had gone by so quickly and here I was, actually done.

It was only four years before that Dad had dropped this scared kid off for college and only 150 yards from where I was now walking. God had been wonderfully faithful to me in this place and these years, as is His nature. So many times in the scriptures God has said to those who trust Him that there is no need to fear because He is with us— wherever we go. That had certainly been my experience. I picked up my step, crossed the quadrangle and headed back to the house for the last time.

(Note: The next chapter begins 15 months later. During these interim 15 months I was an engineer for the

Boeing Company in Seattle and lived in the University district of Seattle, sharing an apartment with Jim Clifton.)

CHAPTER 5
My Year of Sunshine

AS I DROVE TO the end of Stanford's stately Palm Drive and parked my little beat-up sports car, I laughed out loud. I laughed because I had just found myself saying the same thing which I had caught myself saying almost every morning for the past six weeks. "I can't believe this weather!" Because I couldn't. It was the fall of 1964 and I hadn't put the top up on my car even one time. The weather was sunny every day here. This was markedly different from Seattle, my home for the previous five years. The sunshine was a precursor of what this year was to be for me. A very good year. A sunny year. A year about which I would remain sentimental for the rest of my days. A year which would in many ways define the course of the rest of my life.

My journey here had its beginnings the previous December. A friend named Lou had come back home for a family visit over Christmas from his first job out of college. The two of us were out for dinner in Seattle after having both graduated from UW the previous June. Lou shared with me over our meal how he disliked his job and why. He was an engineer working for a major oil company in an isolated little town in the foothills near Bakersfield and was very lonely. Like Lou, I was disliking my first engineering job also but for different reasons than his—I simply did not have enough to do. Even before meeting with him I had spent many coffee breaks praying that I would be able to do something more than be at Boeing from eight to five every Monday through Friday for the next 40 years.

Lou leaned across the table and told me he'd had a good idea. He asked me what I would think about both of us going to Stanford that next fall, enrolling in their two-year program to get our MBA's. I believe that I had to ask him what an MBA was. Long story short, we both applied. And that spring, to my surprise, I received my acceptance. I was surprised because I had driven down in March to meet with the Dean of Admissions for Stanford's Graduate School of Business, and had gotten the distinct impression from him that my odds of getting in were pretty low. He told me they'd already selected students for 190 of the 220 spots, and still had 300 applications to evaluate for the last 30 openings.

The second week in September, my Boeing engineering group pals threw me a fun goodbye party at the Black Angus in Seattle for lunch, and my good buddy, Norm, was working hard to get me drunk. He knew that I'd only had one drink of alcohol in my life to that point, so he kept bringing me glasses of Tom Collins which were very tasty. Driving back to the office with Kathy, a cute secretary I was dating, I remember saying to myself, my head feels a little different. In the parking lot, Kathy gave me a present of a book which I absolutely loved and I was so sad when I accidentally left it on an airplane a few years ago, *One-Hundred and One Famous Poems*. Inside, she had inscribed, "To Joey, from Kath, with love." I had read and quoted some of my favorite poems to her on a date and she knew I liked poetry.

That night after work, I began the drive to Palo Alto. My parents had kindly agreed to help transport some of my belongings, and so we made the drive together— them in their big '56 Olds, and me in my little white TR-2 Triumph with an oven grill for the grill. We stayed overnight in Eugene with my Grandpa and Grandma Kempston, and arrived in Palo Alto the next day. As I was driving through the Siskiyou Mountains right before Lake Shasta, the thought occurred to me that I didn't know anyone there. So I prayed and asked God to give me a good friend. Little did I know how he would answer that hasty prayer with such generosity.

My older sister, Pat, who lived in the area, had found me a place to live at 25893 West Fremont in the Los Altos Hills. It was an older Italian-looking farmhouse on a small amount of acreage. There was a bleached cow skull on the front porch. My roommates were Pete, a doctoral student at Stanford, and Emmett, an engineer at NASA Ames. Emmett and I became good friends. I was a few months shy of 23, and he was 37. He had lost his right arm in a flying accident. During navy flight training he was flying upside down about 100 feet off the ground when he hit a tree. Despite that, he still raced his Porsche and his MG sports cars at Laguna Seca in Monterey occasionally, and was an accomplished tennis and baseball player. He was a strong follower of Jesus, and we had many good talks that year about life, Jesus, and women.

I had a sunny room on the second floor with two windows looking out over the hills. A pepper tree was right outside one of the windows. I had never seen a pepper tree before. I spent the next several days buying a bed and a desk and settling in. I remember buying a can of car wax for the Triumph, and Dad chiding me a bit telling me that I'd better save every penny for the schooling. I had some money stashed away which would last me about halfway through the year, but I wasn't concerned about it. Stanford's tuition was $500 a quarter, or $1500 a year. UW's tuition, by contrast, had only been $100 a quarter.

That Saturday evening, Pete and Emmett drove me on back roads to a great hamburger place in Menlo Park and I began to feel right at home. My sister, Pat, lived only five minutes away, in the pool house of a friendly gas station owner named Louie. I remember the pool, because the first time I dove in, I forgot to take the watch off which my folks had given me for a graduation present 15 months earlier. It drowned.

Sunday morning came, and I went to Peninsula Bible Church (PBC), where Ray Stedman was the well-known pastor. They announced that all college-aged folks were invited to come over to the house of the assistant pastor, Dave Roper, after that evening's service. I made a mental note of that and hoped that I would have time to go. After church I said goodbye to Mom and Dad who were about to begin their drive back to Tacoma. And at five that afternoon, I drove to Stanford for my first class meeting and orientation.

The main speaker was Ernie Arbuckle, the well-loved dean of Stanford's Graduate School of Business. He looked like a good guy—had a cordial way about him. I remember the essence of what he said. He told us to look around at our new classmates and realize that we'd been selected carefully, and that the only reason we would not graduate in two years would be if we pulled the plug on ourselves. He went on to say that we all had the necessary intellect and that we possessed proven leadership ability. He told us that two-thirds of us had played intercollegiate athletics, that half of us had been the president of our living groups as undergrads. And he told us that he was very glad we were there. He ended his remarks by asking us to please knock on the door to his office at least once that next year so he could get to know us even a little. Later, I would take him up on that.

I left the meeting feeling encouraged. This was going to be fun—what a contrast to the negative orientation in my freshman engineering class at the UW. I liked Stanford already!

There was plenty of time afterward to drive from the campus to the evening service at PBC. And I'm so very grateful I went. After church in Dave Roper's home I met two people who would be two of the most significant people God would ever put in my life. The first was a bright, attractive, happy woman in her early twenties named Cherry Gough. She was two weeks into her very first teaching job. We had actually met the year before for half a minute when I'd been in the area for a two-week vacation after graduation before starting my engineering job at Boeing. But this night we were able to talk a bit longer together and actually start an acquaintance.

The other person was a guy with a friendly smile named Craig Duncan. But Craig and I really didn't get a chance to talk after we met, because someone else came up at the same time.

The next morning, however, while standing in the registration line the next morning at the "Biz School," as we called it, I heard a voice behind me call out my name: "Hey, Joe, good morning! Are you ready to do this thing?" I turned around, wondering who in the world it could be, and found that it was Craig Duncan from the night before. I hadn't known that he was going to be a new student, but I was delighted to have a new friend to spend the morning with. Craig had been in a joint program with Claremont College and Stanford, where he studied three years at Claremont, and two years at Stanford to get his undergrad engineering degree. He had grown up in Palo Alto and knew Stanford and the area well.

We had the first of many pleasant lunches together that day under the trees on the sun-filtered back patio of Stanford's Tresidder Student Union. The two of us would enjoy our lunch there almost every day for the next two school years, where we'd often be joined by a few other friends as well.

School officially began the next day. The biz school in those days was at the very front of Stanford's sandstone quadrangle. The quadrangle formed the heart and soul of the University. All the buildings in the quad had red roof tiles, and in the middle of it sat the beautiful Stanford Memorial Chapel. Between the buildings, there were lovely walkways, some gardens and some benches.

I would sit on one of those benches during an hour break mid-morning between classes and drink in the beauty, the blue sky, the sunshine and the feeling. The feeling was gratefulness and joy. I felt so glad and so privileged to be there in the middle of the morning, enjoying being outside. I was so grateful to God for this chance to be back in school again and not sitting at Boeing.

That next Saturday in the late afternoon I was studying in my room when the phone rang. It was Craig, suggesting that the two of us go for a drive around what he said was a scenic valley with pretty hills. He said that he was sure that both of us had done enough studying for the day and that we needed a break. I heartily agreed. So he picked me up a half hour later and we drove on back roads around Portola Valley and Woodside. I was delighted to have this new friend, and somewhere in there realized that God had answered that request I'd made as I was driving through the Siskiyou's ten days earlier. Craig was living with his mother and grandmother and invited me home for a home-cooked meal, which I loved!

Friendship is one of God's greatest gifts to people. The poet, Coleridge, said that "Friendship is a sheltering tree." How true that is. The incredible value of being with someone who likes being with you and shows it. Since my childhood, I had had good friends—in grade school there'd been Neal Dempsey, JL Dejay, Mark Sweeney, and my sister, Judy. In junior high God had given me Jim Medley, Larry Bielmann, Paul Jones, and Rick Wendt. And those carried over into high school. In college there had been Art Volz, Hank Mathews, Tom Watson, and Jim Clifton. And as I write this I'm still in touch with all but two of them, except for the three who have died already.

This friendship with Craig was very much like David and Jonathan's friendship. It was instant and we really enjoyed each other's company. Craig had been a bit lonely since coming to Stanford a few years earlier, and after graduating had spent six months in the army reserve, and the last five summers at a fishing cannery in Alaska. So for both of us, it was a refreshing relationship, and we recognized that right off the bat. He was fun to be with, we laughed a lot and we both kidded each other. We both were sincere, young followers of Jesus. Did we know ourselves well at 22 and 24? (He was close to two years older than me). No, but probably as well as anyone does at that age. Over the years I've learned so much from Craig about being generous and humble and encouraging people.

Stanford's classes were challenging and interesting. I got a D plus on my very first piece of assigned writing—a bit of a shock—but, fortunately, that didn't repeat itself. Classes required both a lot of preparation and class participation. The class participation could be intimidating because there were some very smart people sitting around you. I had never been around cocky New Yorkers before, or soft-spoken folks from the South whose drawls at first disguised their rather imposing intellectual abilities.

One day, about three weeks into school, a bunch of us were sitting at the tables just outside of our building which were there for us to use for coffee breaks and lunch. The subject came up of our scores on the Graduate Record Exam (GRE). Now students getting into graduate level business schools take the GMAT. A couple of guys, when pressed, said that they'd scored on the 90th percentile and 94th percentile. *Wow*, I remembered thinking. I had gotten a 70. So I quietly asked a few more. Their scores were all in the high 80's and low 90's. I didn't ask anybody after that.

But it did make me wonder how I had gotten into Stanford's highly-sought-after graduate program with my 70th percentile GRE score and my modest GPA. It was years later that I figured it out. One of their biggest criteria was leadership. That I had been president of those 3 entities as a senior at UW, and had been the recipient of those two Husky Marching Band awards must have been the reason for my admission to this very good graduate school of business. It certainly wasn't my brains. I've always appreciated Proverbs 16:9 which says that a *man plans his way, but the Lord directs his steps.* Anyway, I was very grateful to be there.

Craig and I happened to be in the main library mid-afternoon a week or so into the fall quarter. Craig liked to study there because it was quiet and comfortable. He interrupted our studying with this: "Joe, would you at all be interested in us taking a couple of girls to the Stanford football game coming up a week from Saturday?" To this day he has always liked sports, and having grown up in Palo Alto, loved Stanford football and basketball. Without thinking much about it, I told him, "Sure." This was actually kind of funny, because I had earlier thought about not dating at all for a year and just really hitting the books hard. However, I had met a few girls at church in the two weeks I'd been there who seemed like they would be fun to get to know.

Several days later he asked me who I was going to take. I had given it some thought and said that I'd either take Cherry Gough, or a girl named Kay, or another named Sue. He knew all three and said immediately that he'd take Cherry if he were me. He said that she was really neat.

So I called Cherry and she said she'd love to. Here's where it gets interesting, and, of course, I didn't know this at the time. Cherry had remembered me from that 30-second meeting a year and three months before, and had actually prayed that we could go out when she'd heard from my sister that I was going to be at Stanford. At that brief encounter the year before, Cherry had been engaged to someone else, someone her mother didn't appreciate for a couple of reasons, and at the time said to Cherry, "Why don't you marry a nice boy like him?" *Wow. Me? Nice?* God is gracious, and so was Cherry's mom.

Our first date was on Saturday, October 10, 1964. Stanford was playing Rice. That first quarter, we had a Saturday morning class from ten until noon. No homework, but very interesting special speakers—Art Linkletter and Viktor Frankl being two of them. Since the game started in the early afternoon, I had thought that Cherry and I could grab some lunch together first, and I asked her if she could have someone drop her off in front of that part of the Quad.

At noon there she was, waiting for me on the steps. I remember being a little surprised at how tall she was, and remarked on that. Sounds awkward, but it wasn't. I told her I had always liked tall girls. We got in my TR and headed down Palm Drive toward the El Camino to find Uncle John's pancake house for lunch. Over our meal we began to get to know one another. She was really pleasant and comfortable to be with. Besides being attractive, with beautiful expressive eyes, there was an innate goodness that I sensed in her. She had an easy smile. Lunch was soon over and we headed to the game. I discovered later that Cherry had been sick earlier in the week, but was determined to make that date. I didn't notice, but she didn't eat much.

We met Craig and his date, Chris Franz, at the stadium gate, bought our tickets and found a good spot in the student section. It was their first date also. As it turned out, both girls were third grade teachers. I don't remember much of the game, just a lot of fun conversations.

On the way home, Cherry mentioned that her mom had said that if I was free I was sure invited over for dinner if I wanted to come. I wasn't about to turn that down. After Cherry had graduated from college the past June, she'd moved back home with her parents and was paying them a nominal amount for room and board. We got to her home in Los Altos, and her dad, Art, immediately asked me to play ping pong in the back yard with him, which I dutifully did. He said we'd play best out of three, and when I'd won the first and third games he asked if we could play best out of five. I figured out what he was doing and let him win the next two so I could talk with Cherry some more. At least that's my version.

So ended our first date, which had been most enjoyable. Thank you, Craig! Honestly, I couldn't wait to see Cherry again. The next day at church I looked for her unsuccessfully, so finally got in the car to drive home. Driving out of the parking lot, I spotted her and pulled over quickly. We stumbled over each other saying exactly the same thing, "I sure had a nice time with you yesterday!" She gave me a plastic pitcher of left-over orange juice from the college group, and I remember it tipped over on the ride home and drenched the upholstery. But I didn't care, I'd gotten to see her and knew we felt the same way.

Cherry told me much later that the weekend previous she'd been on a date with a former Stanford football player now enrolled in law school and had had an uncomfortable time. Imagine, me, the old band guy, beating out a Stanford football player. Joe cool. The weird thing is that this guy showed up 40 years later on 60 Minutes or 20/20 where they disclosed that he'd served prison time for being one of the world's largest manufacturers of the drug, Ecstasy.

A bit about Cherry which I had learned. She was born in Vancouver, BC, Canada, but spent her baby years in eastern Canada during World War Two, and moved with her parents and little sister to California when she was in the fifth grade. Because her folks had moved around a bit, she'd been the new kid on the block and in the classroom many times. I found out she was pretty coordinated. She'd not only won first place in the San Mateo County jump roping competition in the sixth grade, she'd also won a prize in the volleyball serve contest. She could waterski on one ski and she knew how to fly fish. Cherry had graduated from Los Altos High School four years earlier, and from Westmont College in Santa Barbara the previous June. She was now in her first year of teaching in East Palo Alto, a city known for its crime and poverty. She had her hands full in her third grade classroom with 34 children.

Tuesday night rolled around, and by eight I was done studying, so I called Cherry and asked her if there was any chance I could pick her up in twenty minutes and take her out for a cup of coffee. This was before Starbucks and coffee shops, so I took her to a Denny's on El Camino. We had another great time of getting more acquainted.

I really liked who she was — a great mix of goodness, kindness, sincerity and beauty, and I was more than intrigued.

Heading home, we had a slight adventure. Going through old downtown Los Altos, my not-so-trusty Triumph decided to lose a bolt out of the ring gear in the rear end, and so the car locked up. It'd go ten feet forward or ten feet backward, but that was it. We pushed the car over to the curb with the help of the guys in the car behind us, but I was pretty puzzled about my next course of action.

That's when Cherry had the good sense to suggest we call her dad. She called him from a nearby phone booth, and he was there in ten minutes. When I described what the car was doing, he handed me a pair of overalls, and told me to get under the car—that the problem was in the rear end housing. He handed me a "spanner." (Even though he'd been out of Canada for 11 years now, he still called a wrench by its British term.) Sure enough, there was a bolt which had come out and was stuck in the gear housing. I took it out, he drove Cherry home, and—now that the TR was drivable again—I drove it home. Bought a new bolt the next day to replace the beat up old one. As it turned out, Cherry still had a lot of prep for her class for the next day which she had to work on when she finally got home.

When I called Cherry a few days later, she let me know that her dad would like to play tennis with me the next Saturday afternoon and then could I possibly come over there for dinner? So that Saturday, Art and I played tennis and it was a repeat of the ping pong thing. We'd agreed to play the best of three sets. I won the first two, so it quickly morphed into the best of five. Anyway, to make sure I wasn't going to be playing tennis until 9 that night, he managed to win the next three. Don't know how that happened.

But it was so good to be there in their home again. Cherry's mom, Jo, was a great cook, and I enjoyed watching Cherry help her mom bring out food to the picnic table. She was wearing jeans and a checkered red shirt.

The following night my TR-2 wasn't running - can't remember why - and so I borrowed Emmett's red 1959 MGA roadster to go to church. After church there was a "singspiration" at Craig's (something we did after evening church in the '60's), and I asked Cherry if I could give her a ride home from that. Since it was still nice and warm outside, I asked her if she knew a place with a view so we could just park and talk. Cherry suggested Foothill College, and it was perfect. We found a knoll high on a hill, and were chatting away when a cop showed up and asked if we were okay. We assured him that we were, and he said he was only asking because we were parked sidewise in the middle of the road at the top of an incline. Oops.

So that's how Cherry and I got started. She liked me a lot, too, and I began getting a card or two from her in the mail every week. She was more expressive through her words in those cards than she was verbally. I bought cards for her from a little shop down on Main Street in Los Altos. Our dates were always doing free things, walking, talking, seeing things. We both remember eating at Round Table Pizza after church one night on First Street in Los Altos—the place is still there.

I'll never forget the first time we kissed. It was on a Sunday evening in her parents' living room. We'd been going out for three weeks. Cherry's old boyfriend from college had come through town that weekend and had brought her a present of a record for her birthday. She wanted me to listen to it with her, so I sat on a hassock right next to her and she sat on the floor right below me. As *The Girl from Ipanema* started playing, Cherry looked up at me. I looked back into her beautiful hazel eyes and we stayed locked in that inviting gaze through the whole song. When the song was through, I leaned down and gave her a long lingering kiss. Have always loved that song. And have always been properly grateful for her old boyfriend bringing her the record. I don't imagine he anticipated Cherry enjoying his record quite that way, but, what the heck. Win a few, lose a few.

One weekend that fall we drove down to Carmel on Highway 101 in her blue and white '56 Ford, and I fondly recall driving through those fragrant Eucalyptus groves just after the turnoff to San Juan Bautista. Eucalyptus trees were new to me. Carmel was magical fun, and we loved taking our time strolling up and down the quaint streets and enjoying the sandy beach. I did notice that

Cherry got quite tired walking back up Ocean Avenue to our car afterwards.

Every once in a while the college group at church would sponsor what they called a "Seminar Three." Dave Roper would arrange for a special speaker gifted in speaking to non-Christian university audiences. The idea was that you could bring a friend who was not a follower of Jesus, knowing that the gospel would be presented well and in an interesting fashion.

One of these Seminar Three's was held on a Tuesday in early November, the day after my birthday. I had brought a friend, and because of that, had told Cherry that I wouldn't be able to hang around her that evening. However, there was an attractive and outgoing girl present who worked at the biz school at Stanford. Both Craig and I had become friends with her. Knowing that it had been my birthday the day before, she brought me some home baked chocolate chip cookies. She also seemed to be wherever I was that evening, and Cherry noticed.

When I got home that night, Cherry called and asked if, even though it was late and a school night, could I come over to talk about something. (Found out later that her dad had advised strongly against calling me.) I immediately sensed what it was going to be about. Sure enough, she had noticed the girl, and in a very straightforward manner asked me just where she, Cherry, stood. I assured her, truthfully, that what she had observed had not been instigated by me at all, and that I was not interested in anyone but her. I remember leaving the house to get in my car, and thinking to myself, "Joe, she isn't the kind of person you can ever lead on or play games with. She is way too sensitive, honest and good. So do the right thing."

Just a block from her house and because the hour was late, I chose to roll through a stop sign. The policeman who was waiting for someone to do that very thing turned on his flashing red light. He noticed my Washington license plate and asked whether or not I was familiar with the area. I assured him that I was not, and he let me off.

Classes at Stanford were challenging, but enjoyable. Driving to school each morning before class began at eight was really fun. Top down, passing fruit trees in and among the hills, the air smelling good. It was exhilarating. Usually I would drink my breakfast: two raw eggs in a blender with some milk and chocolate syrup, sometimes with an additive called Tiger's milk, to which Emmett had introduced me. Back then raw eggs weren't blamed for salmonella, which I hadn't heard of anyway. One Monday morning I opened the refrigerator door to discover that I'd run out of eggs and milk, so I got in the car having eaten nothing. And I was really hungry. Fortunately, I discovered a piece of left-over pepperoni pizza from Friday night sitting in the pocket of my car door. Pizza never tasted so good.

Having Craig for a pal wasn't just great simply because he was such a great guy. He not only knew the area very well, he also took the time to acquaint me with it. He showed me picturesque Lake Lagunita, now sadly only a memory, and introduced me to the Peninsula Creamery, which to this day serves the best burgers, fries and shakes on the peninsula. Over our daily lunches, we would commiserate over school together and talk about our love lives. He was still dating Chris.

One of those days, walking over to lunch, he asked me if I'd kissed Cherry yet. I don't know exactly why, but to me Craig was this spiritual giant kind of guy, and I didn't want to offend him and didn't want to appear shallow, so I lied and said that I hadn't. He grinned maliciously at me and said that he'd kissed Chris the night before. Whereupon, I told him that I actually had kissed Cherry also. He started laughing and teased me about being a liar for the next three weeks. Indeed, I had been—both shallow and a liar.

Craig and I had a couple of other friends from the biz school we studied with and hung out with to varying degrees—Steve Anderson, a big tall handsome guy who was married to Myrna. Steve had graduated from Seattle Pacific University. The other guy was Dave Paup. Dave and I had been in school together for three years of high school and he had gone to Oregon State. He was married to Judi, another Clover Park classmate of ours.

Sometime that fall, Craig, Steve and I began meeting inside Stanford's Memorial Chapel weekly to pray together for a few minutes. We had to pray pretty loudly because sometimes there would be a music student playing triple forte on the pipe organ. On at least a couple of occasions the organist would stop unexpectedly, and one of us would be caught praying loudly. Must have sounded like college holy rollers.

Another guy who became a good friend to both Craig and me was Len Sunukjian. Len had graduated from Westmont with Cherry, and was on a one-year Masters' program at Stanford to get a teaching credential. Len would come over to my farmhouse sometimes and we'd lift weights together. Afterwards, we'd eat tacos, which he taught me how to cook. Loved those tacos. Still do. Len was also my first Armenian friend. He had grown up in Pasadena.

Thanksgiving that year is a great memory for me. In the morning right after breakfast I lit a fire in the fireplace in our living room, set up some cushions against the wall and began reading a book by Milton Friedman, the famous University of Chicago economist. Very cozy. Late morning I turned the radio on and listened to the Army Navy game. Roger Staubach was Navy's quarterback. Late afternoon I drove over to Cherry's and enjoyed eating her mom's delicious turkey dinner. It was the first time I had ever eaten sweet potatoes that I liked. Her candied yams were delicious. This was the first year I had not celebrated Thanksgiving in my parents' home, but it had been a memorable, good day.

Before school broke for Christmas and I headed back home to Tacoma, Cherry and I shared a special moment in her folk's kitchen. We were home there alone, and just chatting away. She was probably doing lesson plans. I found a little piece of paper, and wrote on it, "You're the one," and gave it to her. She still has that note today. At the time, I think I wanted to tell her that I loved her, but I was saving those words until the day when I really knew for sure and would ask her to marry me.

Soon we had finals and Christmas break. The night before I was to drive to Tacoma, I took Cherry out to a romantic restaurant across the El Camino from Stanford's stadium where we ate dinner by candlelight. She doesn't remember this. To me it had been a stunning evening, with Christmas decorations and candles in the dining area.

The next morning, a fellow classmate and I took off for Seattle. We'd arranged to return a rent-a car to Seattle, so we could travel for free. The rental outfit provided us with gas money. We were trying to make good time and I got a ticket for speeding on I-5 somewhere between Dunnigan and Arbuckle. Further north in the Siskiyous it began to snow. It snowed all the way to Tacoma and what normally was a 14-hour trip took 20 hours. Arrived at my parents at three in the morning. So much for making good time.

One night after Christmas I caught Dad in the living room and asked him a question. They'd been married at that point for almost 30 years and I knew that he and mom were still deeply in love. He adored her. Dad had always steered me straight when I asked him for advice, so I asked him how he knew mom was the one back when he was dating her. He thought for a minute and said that the question required some thought and he'd get back to me. The next day he told me that it wasn't logic or anything like that—he just knew. He loved her and he just knew. I didn't know what to do with that because I think I was looking for something more specific, but I thanked him.

I returned to California on December 31st. Drove down with my friend, Lou, the guy who had suggested Stanford in the first place. He hadn't been accepted, and was still working for the oil company. But, we did drive down in his new black Porsche which he let me drive part of the time.

In February after lifting weights and eating tacos with Len one day, he asked me casually if I would like to visit his Young Life club some time. He knew that I had been helping with the junior high department at PBC. Len had been volunteering in one of the Young Life clubs in Palo Alto that year. I gave it a quick, "Why not?" The area director called me the next night. "Joe, this is Bob Reeverts with Young Life. I understand you want to be a Young Life leader." Well, that wasn't exactly, or even anywhere close to what I had said, but we did end up arranging for me to visit his Young Life club that next evening. It was the club for Los Altos High. I did—and that week was the beginning of Young Life involvement which continues to this day. Bob would be a mentor in my life for the next four decades.

Cherry and I were seeing more and more of each other as the winter moved along. She had moved into an apartment with a roommate, mostly due to my urging her to do so. There was one very special Saturday there when her roommate, Susan, was gone for the weekend. I came over mid-morning on a Saturday and studied there the entire day, with Cherry making me both lunch and dinner. She was wearing an orange and brown dress, I recall, and I absolutely loved that day. It felt like playing house and really made me think about what being married to her would feel like. And I honestly did get a lot of studying done that day.

Over spring break, my pal and former roommate from the Northwest, Jim Clifton, visited for a few days. Jim was in his first year of medical school at UW. During his visit, we drove the TR up to Big Basin one day, and discovered on the map that there was a 13-mile dirt road, in very bad shape, which led to Highway 1 on the coast. The map very clearly indicated that the road was impassable in winter. But winter was over—it was March—and so we thought we'd take our chances. That drive was such a kick. Kept the car in 2nd gear, a great gear in that car, almost the entire time, skidding around corners playing race car driver, because we knew nobody would be coming uphill the other way. Once we rounded a blind corner really pushing it, and just managed to slide between a log down across part of the road and a huge mud puddle. We got to the coast in muddy fine shape. That was a drive I'll never forget.

That weekend I was scheduled to take kids to my first Young Life weekend camp at Mt Hermon, so I asked Jim if he would spend some time with Cherry and get acquainted with her while I was gone. They had a great time, and he left me a long letter letting me know how special he thought she was. He had written the letter because he was heading back to Seattle and would be gone by the time I returned from the weekend. His opinion meant very much to me, because he knew me really well. I found out later that he and Cherry had written the letter together!

As school resumed, I read an article in the Stanford Daily reporting how the student body president, Scott, had just returned from attending the prayer breakfast in Washington DC. He had really liked it and been challenged by it. Sensing an opening for the gospel, I knocked on the door of his office the next day, introduced myself, and told him I'd read the article, and asked him what he would think about some of us starting a weekly casual lunch just opening one of the gospels together and reading about Jesus. Maybe he could get a guy or two to come and I would do the same. He loved the idea.

So the next week we started a bag lunch picnic on the lawn which went until the end of the school year. Craig, Steve and I each brought someone, and Scott did also. Years later, Scott would confide in Steve, (who would end up later running the New York office for KPMG) that those lunches spent discussing Jesus were a key part of the process in his decision to begin following Jesus.

Also that spring a friend of Cherry's family, Dick Vogel, asked me if I would like to run with him several times a week. I had never run before, but had always wanted to. Dick had been a half-miler at San Jose State and in the army. That spring he and I met at Middlefield Park several times a week in the late afternoon to run together. That sparked my life-long passion for running. Often I'd drive to Cherry's after, and she would remark how red faced and wiped-out I looked. Indeed. Dick ran my legs off.

Meanwhile, Cherry was going through a tough time. That winter, she had been more tired and more tired—sometimes simply exhausted. As it turned out, mononucleosis had come on full force, and the doctor told her that she needed to leave her teaching job, move back home, and do bed rest for the next six weeks. This was a very difficult time for her—leaving her classroom in April instead of June and having to stay in bed all day every day. Pretty depressing. As it turned out, she'd probably had mono since her junior year of college. I felt so badly for her. This is probably TMI, but we even gave up kissing, since mono could be spread through kissing. They even referred to it as "the kissing disease." If I'd contracted it, I would have had to drop out of school, and Vietnam would have been a distinct possibility.

Meanwhile, as I was juggling studies, Young Life, running, and the junior high group at church, the real thing constantly on my mind was Cherry. *Should I marry her?* I wanted to, but I knew marriage was permanent, and was a huge deal, and didn't want to move ahead of God's plans for my life. I didn't want to mess up.

So two or three times a week for perhaps a month in the evening I would head out into our backyard, and sit on one of the bales of hay there, looking out at the hills and up to the sky, and pray. My prayer was pretty much the same every time. "Heavenly father, thank you that I can pray to you the same way that David did 3000 years ago. He spent so many nights outside at night looking at the same stars I'm seeing right now. Thank you for hearing me. I need to know whether it's okay with you if I ask Cherry to marry me. I have no idea how you will let me know, but I pledge to not go ahead until you give me your go-ahead."

I waited. One Sunday afternoon, I had been asked to go with the youth group from PBC to Natural Bridges State Park in Santa Cruz. Dave Roper, from PBC, was someone I really respected, and Dave was on the outing also. Late in the afternoon, I sat down next to him and asked him what he would think of the idea of me asking Cherry to marry me. His answer was more encouraging than he would ever know. He said simply that I would be very fortunate to marry her and that she would be very fortunate to marry me.

I continued to pray and wait. I visited Cherry regularly, and the doctor said that she could go on a drive once a week. So we did that on weekends.

Saturday, May 22nd rolled around, and as I woke that morning, the sun was streaming in the window—the window with that pepper tree outside. I felt this strange and wonderful sense of peace. God was letting me know that Cherry and me being married was definitely in his plans. It was honestly as though it was written on the walls of the room. "Go ahead, ask her. You've got my ok!"

To say I was delighted and excited was an understatement. I called her to see if she could go for a drive with me that afternoon. She said she could. When I picked her up, I had selected in my mind a perfect place to ask her. It was in one of Stanford's out-of-the-way gardens. The garden even had one of those swinging chairs for two people. We sat down and I put my arm around her, my heart racing wildly, and that's when I blew it big time. I said, "Cherry, uh, Cherry, would you, would you like to go over to the student union building and have a coke with me?" All the way over to the student union building I kept telling myself that I was the biggest chicken I had ever met. Talking to Cherry later, she didn't have a clue what was going on.

Well, the next day my resolve returned. I headed to her place late afternoon. It had been a particularly hard day for Cherry and so her mom had asked some friends to visit her. She told me later that two girl friends had asked that afternoon if we were going to get engaged soon. Cherry had told them she thought it would probably be a long time.

When I arrived she still had one guest, a mutual friend named John, and I couldn't wait for him to leave, which he took his sweet time in doing. The minute he left, I suggested we head out to her backyard and hang out there because it was such a beautiful afternoon. She was talking about something—I have no idea what. I just interrupted her and asked, "Cherry, will you marry me?"

We've often laughed since, because I don't think she said anything back, but gave me a fierce hug and wouldn't let go. Afterwards we sat down at the picnic table in her backyard, prayed and asked God to be right in the middle of our marriage. Wow. I'd done it. We'd done it. God had done it. So happy. We even set a date for some time the third week in July.

That night Cherry's mom called to congratulate me and said that they were so pleased and excited for us. She asked if we could change the date to later in August so Jo-Anne, Cherry's sister could come. She was going on a short term missions trip to Peru. I said that would be fine.

And, by the way, Craig had asked Chris to marry him just a few weeks before. What a double date that had been the previous October 10th! They would be married in July, a month ahead of us.

We only had two or three weeks left before I would go back to Seattle for a summer job I'd lined up at Boeing. Somewhere in that period of time, the two of us settled on Ephesians 2:10 for our "life" verse together.

"For we are God's handiwork, created in Christ Jesus to do good works, which God prepared in advance for us to do." Sounds kind of quaint, but God really did give us that verse as a fact, as a promise, and as a guide. And we've been able to do many of those things which he planned ahead of time for us to do.

I was pretty much out of money at this point in the college year. Hadn't eaten out in ages, and had bought a lot of hot dogs, cans of tuna, and bread to stretch out my money as far as it could go. I even had to borrow $85 from Cherry to get my steering aligned for the trip home. Then

I sold my weight set to a fellow student for gas money for the trip—a whopping $25.

I drove out of town early that last morning of this ever-so-special year. My roommate, Emmett, always so kind, had taken me out to breakfast. I was going to make it as far as Eugene and stay with Grandpa and Grandma Kempston. Coming down a long grade in the Siskiyous, the TR engine died. I prayed immediately as I pulled over. Lord, help this to be a simple thing. It was. The accelerator cable had come disconnected somehow. I reattached that and continued on. About fifty miles outside of Eugene a steady rain started. I had my top down, but just kept going, because when you're going fast, the windshield gets rid of most of it. I rolled into my grandparents place right on time, and broke my personal record in putting the top back up.

How kind God had been to me this wonderful year! I had met the two people who would be my very best friends for my whole life. And I was going to marry one of them in two short months. Our wedding would be the tenth I would be in in the past three years. I'd been introduced to Young Life and have been involved deeply ever since, sharing Jesus with young friends. I'd even began the habit of running, which I still do today.

As Jesus once remarked, "I am the light of the world. Whoever follows me will never walk in darkness but will have the light of life." This was indeed a year of sunshine and light for me. And I'll be forever grateful.

Epilogue

CHERRY AND I REPEATED our marriage vows to each other two months later on a pleasant Saturday afternoon in Palo Alto, August 21, 1965. We honeymooned first in Carmel for two nights and then, as big spenders for the next five days, in the tent cabins at Yosemite's Curry Village for $2 a night. (Just checked and as of right now, 2020, they are $143/night.) I had always wanted to visit Yosemite, because growing up as a kid, there was a picture of the Yosemite valley hanging over my bed. It was even more beautiful than I had imagined.

Back home, Cherry and I rented a small, furnished apartment just off the El Camino in Palo Alto where we lived the next year. Cherry continued teaching 3rd grade at Kavenaugh Elementary in East Palo Alto while I finished up my second-year MBA studies at Stanford.

After graduating in June 1966 we made the move to LaCanada (and Pasadena) in Southern California where I worked for Jet Propulsion Laboratory as a systems engineer on a spacecraft which did a flyby of Mars in 1969. Our David was born in 1967 while there. The next year Cherry and I moved back to Northern California where I worked for Itek Corporation in Palo Alto for three years as a product marketing manager. Our family continued to grow. In early 1970 we adopted Kristie, and later that year

Cherry gave birth to Lisa. We were now a happy family of five.

Meanwhile, the ministry of Young Life (YL) continued to capture our hearts. I had started the YL club at Gunn High during my second year at Stanford, even though I didn't have much background in YL. It was a struggle, but Dave Roper, a wonderful mentor, helped me with ideas for talks. He was a real lifesaver. When we moved to LaCanada, Cherry and I volunteered in the Pasadena High club as junior leaders and climbed rapidly up the learning curve. Now that we were back in Northern California, I volunteered to be the senior leader in the Homestead High YL club in Sunnyvale. After being there six months, I used my accrued vacation to take kids from that club to Malibu, the YL camp in Canada.

The job at Itek required a significant amount of travel—all over the mainland US, Hawaii and Europe. Whenever possible, I scheduled my trips around Homestead High's YL club. Kids were being introduced to Jesus and their lives were being changed. To minimize my time away from our family, sometimes I'd leave the YL club, head for the airport, and take the all-night "red-eye" plane to the east coast to conduct business.

On one of those all-night flights, I drank too much coffee and couldn't sleep. All I could think about was the big YL club I had just left and how much I cared about those kids. I realized that I was certainly decent at my job, evidenced by generous pay raises, but in the early morning hours on that flight it became clear to me that what really grabbed my heart was being with those kids, loving them, and letting them know that God loved them way more than I did. When I returned home a day later, I asked Cherry what she would think about the idea of me leaving the business world in a year and joining the full-time YL staff for maybe a decade. I was 28 at the time and I was thinking that I could do it until I hit 40. I cautioned her that it would mean a significant reduction in salary. Cherry replied back something like—"Hey, I'm with you. If that is what God is calling us to, then let's do it."

So 15 months later, after paying off hospital and doctor bills for Lisa's birth, the second mortgage on our house, and the $2000 loan I had taken to get through Stanford we made the switchover. We discovered it wasn't to be just for a decade, but for 33 years.

Our first YL assignment was right there in Sunnyvale, Santa Clara and Cupertino for three years, then it was on to San Jose for two, Spokane for eleven, and Monterey for seventeen. Our fourth child, Shaun, came along during our Spokane years. Interestingly enough, he was born exactly eleven years after Lisa—same date, same week day, and same time at night. We had always wanted a fourth child and he finally showed up!

So for Cherry and me, life didn't end up being about engineering or business. It was clearly about Jesus and kids—four of our own kids, and through Young Life, countless more. And we experienced God's unfailing love and faithfulness through all of it. We counted it up once and through the years we had over 20 people live with us at different times, or live in our house when we were away on YL assignments, camps or training. I led YL clubs and trained leaders for well over 40 years, while Cherry befriended YL leaders and committee people. The two of us are currently volunteer leaders in the Capernaum YL club (for special needs kids) here in Gig Harbor where we have lived since 2003. Three of our children have served as volunteer leaders in YL. It was our privilege to be part of teams at YL camps numerous summers in California, Colorado and Canada. In later years I took almost two dozen trips to former Soviet Union countries to help train YL staff there. We still are in touch with many of the kids from the clubs through the years. Some of those "kids" are in their sixties now. Hardly a day goes by that we don't get an e-mail, text, Facebook message, or phone call from one of them. All of this was so much more than either Cherry or I anticipated when we began.

Paul's words to one of the churches in modern day Turkey proved so true in our lives—"God can do anything, you know — far more than you could ever imagine or guess or request in your wildest dreams! He does it not by pushing us around but by working within us, his Spirit gently and deeply within us." (Ephesians 3:20-21, Msg)

A final story with which to end. In the spring of 1978 while living in Spokane, David, our oldest, was a ten-year-old fifth grader. He and I had decided to run Bloomsday — soon to be the third largest fun run in the U.S. That year it was 8.5 miles long with 5000 people signed up to run in it. David and I put in a lot of miles together in practice and even ran the course once ahead of time to increase our confidence that we could do it. Up to this point I had always been the stronger runner of the two of us. We felt prepared.

But on race day, at the top of a steep hill around mile six, I said to David that I needed to go slower for a bit to recover my breath. I urged him to go ahead and told him that I would meet him at the finish line. He took off at a good pace; I took off at a slower one. Then, to my surprise, just a half mile ahead, I discovered him waiting for me at the side of the road. As he got in the flow of runners beside me, I asked him why he had waited for me instead of just meeting me at the finish line. His grinning reply was classic. "Dad, we're in this thing together." I smiled and thought to myself that those are probably words our heavenly Father wants to hear from us — that we understand and recognize that we are in this life together with him — that the race of life in which every created being is engaged makes no sense at all without him. And that life with him makes all the sense in the world. It sure has for me.

Joe Kempston
January 2020

Made in the USA
San Bernardino, CA
08 April 2020